# I JUST CAN'T FORGIVE THAT!

# I JUST CAN'T FORGIVE THAT!

GET YOUR LIFE BACK AFTER BEING HURT

## KEITH WEST

Woodhane
Stubble
PUBLISHING

Published by Woodhane Stubble Publishing, Bellevue, Nebraska

ISBN: 979-8-9939194-2-3

First Edition

Cover design by Keith West

The information and advice in this book are based on the author's experience and are intended for informational purposes only. This book is not intended as a substitute for professional counseling, therapy, or medical advice. If you are experiencing severe emotional distress, trauma, or mental health concerns, please seek help from a qualified professional.

If you are in an unsafe situation involving domestic violence, abuse, or any threat to your safety, please contact the National Domestic Violence Hotline (1-800-799-7233) or local emergency services immediately. The principles in this book are designed for processing past hurts and setting healthy boundaries, they are not a substitute for professional intervention in dangerous situations.

*This book is dedicated to the hundreds of people who have trusted me to walk alongside them through their journey toward forgiveness.*

*Your courage inspired this book.*

*Your freedom is why it exists.*

# CONTENTS

# FOREWORD

## How to Use This Book

This book exists because hundreds of people trusted me to walk alongside them through forgiveness. If you're holding this book, you're joining that journey. Whether you're reading it alone, working through it with a counselor, or you're a pastor looking for resources to help others, welcome. Freedom is possible. Let me show you how.

**If you're not sure forgiveness is even possible,** start with the Introduction and Part I. These chapters will help you understand what forgiveness actually means (and what it doesn't mean) and show you why staying stuck is costing you more than you realize.

**If you already understand forgiveness but feel stuck in anger,** skip straight to Part II. Chapter 9 will help you understand why anger feels so powerful, and Chapters 10-11 give you practical tools to break free.

**If you're working through this with a counselor or in a group,** each chapter ends at a natural stopping point for discussion or reflection.

**About Chapter 12:** The final chapter explores the foundation of forgiveness from a Christian perspective. Your forgiveness journey is complete without reading it. This chapter is for those who want to explore the deeper "why" behind what you've learned.

**A note about the tools in Chapter 10:** You don't need to use all of them. Find what resonates with your personality and situation. One or two techniques practiced consistently will be more effective than trying to use everything at once. Feel free to revisit this section as you work through your forgiveness journey, the tools you need from this section may change over time.

**Most importantly:** This isn't a book to read once and put on a shelf. Keep it nearby. Come back to the chapters you need when you need them. Write in the margins. Highlight what resonates. Make it yours.

Forgiveness is a journey, not a destination. Let this book be your companion along the way.

# INTRODUCTION

## When Forgiveness Seems Impossible

You picked up this book because there's something you just can't forgive.

Maybe you've told yourself a hundred times that you should "let it go" or "move on." Maybe you haven't thought about that situation for a long time, then the title of this book brought it to the front of your mind. Maybe well-meaning friends have quoted scripture at you or suggested you're holding yourself back by not forgiving.

But you know what they don't understand... some things feel genuinely unforgivable.

Let me tell you about Gary and Cathy Hagen.

## When the Unthinkable Happens

Gary and Cathy were living an ordinary life in California when their world shattered in an instant. Their son was killed by a drunk driver. Not injured. Not hurt. Killed.

Imagine that phone call. The knock at the door. The moment when everything you thought you knew about safety, about fairness, about how the world works gets ripped away from you. All because of one person's careless choice.

At that moment, Gary Hagen knew one thing with absolute certainty... he would never, ever forgive the person who did this. How could he? How could anyone expect him to? This wasn't some accident or misunderstanding. Someone chose to get behind the wheel drunk and destroyed his family.

The anger felt right. It felt justified. It felt like the only appropriate response to an unthinkable tragedy.

For years, that anger sustained Gary and Cathy. It gave them energy when grief would have left them collapsed. It gave them focus when everything else felt chaotic. It validated that what happened mattered, that their son mattered.

The drunk driver was caught, tried, and sentenced. Justice was served, at least in the legal sense.

But Gary and Cathy were still stuck. Still angry. Still replaying that phone call, that moment when their lives changed forever. The driver was paying his debt to society, but they were paying a debt too... in sleepless nights, in relationships strained by constant anger, in the way their son's memory was becoming tangled up with rage and bitterness.

Something had to change.

### The Impossible Choice

Here's what nobody tells you about forgiveness... sometimes it starts not with compassion for the person who hurt you, but with exhaustion over what that hurt is doing to you.

Gary Hagen didn't wake up one morning feeling generous toward his son's killer. He wasn't even fully aware that something had been changing slowly inside him. What changed? He woke up tired. Tired of being angry. Tired of the way that anger was stealing what was left of his life. Tired of being defined by the worst thing that had ever happened to him.

So Gary and Cathy made a decision that seemed impossible to everyone who knew them, including themselves. They reached out through a victim-offender mediation program. They asked to meet the man who killed their son.

Not because he deserved it. Not because they felt sorry for him. Not because they wanted to let him off the hook.

But because they needed to be free.

### The Meeting That Changed Everything

I wish I could tell you exactly what happened in that room when Gary and Cathy sat across from their son's killer. I wasn't there. But I know it wasn't a Hollywood moment where everyone hugged and all was forgiven.

What I know is that something shifted.

I can't tell you what they thought of him after that meeting. Maybe he stayed a monster in their minds. Maybe not. What I know is that something shifted... not about him, but about whether they needed him to change, to apologize, or to be anything other than what he was before they could move forward. They could leave him exactly as he was... and still choose freedom for themselves.

Gary described forgiveness as the only way he could move forward without being destroyed by anger. Not because the driver deserved forgiveness, but because Gary deserved to be free from the prison of perpetual rage.

They didn't just meet once. Gary and Cathy began speaking with the man regularly. Eventually, they started speaking together at schools about drunk driving. The three of them... victims and perpetrator...

working together to prevent other families from experiencing their tragedy.

And here's the remarkable thing, they weren't alone.

## A Pattern Emerges

The Rodriguez family faced something even more difficult. Their loved one was murdered during a robbery. Not a momentary lapse in judgment. A deliberate act of violence that destroyed their sense of safety and stole someone precious from them.

Like Gary and Cathy, they knew with certainty that forgiveness was impossible. The murderer showed no remorse initially. There was no momentary lapse of judgement to understand. This was deliberate evil, and evil didn't deserve forgiveness.

For years, they carried that burden. Every day was colored by the violence that had been done to them. Every news story about crime brought it all back. Every family gathering was marked by the empty chair, the missing voice, the person who should have been there.

The murderer was convicted and sentenced, but that didn't ease their pain. If anything, the trial made it worse, forcing them to relive the details over and over again.

Then, like the Hagens, they were offered an opportunity to meet with their loved one's killer through a victim-offender mediation program. Their first reaction? Absolute refusal. Why would they want to see that person? What could he possibly say that would matter?

But something was eating at them. The same exhaustion the Hagens had felt. The anger that had felt so righteous, so necessary, was consuming their lives. They realized they had become prisoners of a moment no one should ever have to live through... and they didn't know how to honor their loved one's memory while still learning to live again.

The meeting was difficult. Painful. The murderer had found some measure of remorse over the years, but that almost made it harder. If he had remained defiant, evil, inhuman... it would have been easier to keep hating him.

Instead, they found themselves face-to-face with someone who had caused immeasurable damage... and somehow, in that meeting, something shifted inside them. Not about him. About their own ability to stop being consumed by what he'd done.

The Rodriguez family described the process as freeing them from the burden of hatred they had been carrying. They didn't excuse what he had done. They didn't minimize their loss. But they chose to release themselves from the exhausting work of maintaining constant anger toward him.

### What These Stories Reveal

Here's what's remarkable about both of these families... they weren't motivated by trying to be heroes or saints. They weren't following some religious obligation to forgive. They were simply people who discovered that forgiveness wasn't about the person who hurt them... it was about reclaiming their own lives.

Neither family forgave because the person deserved it. They forgave because staying angry was destroying them. Because carrying hatred had become a burden they were tired of bearing. Because they needed to be free.

In both cases, forgiveness didn't mean forgetting what happened or pretending it was okay. It didn't mean letting the person off the hook or saying the crime didn't matter. It meant refusing to let those tragic events continue to define and consume their daily lives.

### The Question This Raises

Now, I want you to think about your situation. The thing you can't forgive. The person who hurt you. The betrayal that still stings. The injustice that still makes your blood boil.

I'm not suggesting it's murder or drunk driving. It might be. But it probably isn't.

Maybe it's a spouse who had an affair. Maybe it's a parent who was never there for you. Maybe it's a friend who betrayed your trust. Maybe it's a boss who sabotaged your career. Maybe it's someone who spread lies about you. Maybe it's something else entirely.

Here's a question... If they found freedom by choosing to forgive murder and drunk driving, would you be willing to take a step and explore whether that same freedom might be possible for you?

I'm not asking you to minimize your pain or pretend your situation doesn't matter. Your pain is real. What happened to you was wrong. What I am asking is this... what is staying angry costing you?

## What This Book Will and Won't Do

This book isn't going to tell you that what happened to you was okay. It wasn't.

It's not going to tell you that you should trust people who have proven themselves untrustworthy. You shouldn't.

It's not going to suggest that forgiveness means becoming a doormat or letting people walk all over you. It doesn't.

What this book will do is show you a path forward that doesn't require you to carry the weight of anger and resentment for the rest of your life. A path that gives you back your peace, your energy, and your freedom to choose how you want to spend your emotional resources.

In this book, you'll discover there's a process to forgiveness. Steps that people naturally move through... and places where people naturally get stuck. You'll learn what forgiveness actually is (and what it isn't).

You'll get practical tools to break the anger cycles that keep you trapped. And you'll find a way forward that doesn't require the person who hurt you to participate at all.

Forgiveness, as you'll discover, isn't about them. It's about you.

It's about leaving behind anger that once protected you but now imprisons you.

It's about reclaiming your life from the people who hurt you.

Let's begin.

# PART I

## I JUST CAN'T FORGIVE THAT

# 1

## YOUR SITUATION

Y ou picked up this book because there's something, or someone, you just can't forgive.

Maybe you've tried before. Maybe you've told yourself you should "let it go" or "move on." Maybe you've prayed about it, talked to friends about it, or even have seen a counselor about it. But you're still stuck.

Struggling to forgive doesn't make you a bad person. You're human, and someone hurt you in a way that matters.

### It Doesn't Have to Be Murder

The stories in the introduction were dramatic. Murder and drunk driving are both unthinkable tragedies. Your situation might not be anything like that. It doesn't have to be.

Maybe your spouse had an affair, and now you can't imagine trusting anyone again.

Maybe a parent abandoned you emotionally, leaving you to figure out life without the guidance and support you needed.

Maybe a friend spread your secrets or betrayed your confidence when you were most vulnerable, and now you question every relationship.

Maybe a boss or coworker sabotaged your career, stealing opportunities that were rightfully yours.

Maybe someone falsely accused you of something you didn't do, and the lie spread before you could defend yourself.

Maybe someone broke a promise that changed the course of your life.

Maybe you experienced abuse or neglect as a child that shaped how you see yourself and the world.

Maybe someone you trusted took advantage of you financially, leaving you not just poorer but feeling foolish.

Maybe it was a series of smaller hurts that accumulated over time until you couldn't take anymore.

The specific situation doesn't matter. What matters is that it hurt you. What matters is that it's still with you, still affecting you. What matters is that somewhere along the way, those words crossed your mind or came out of your mouth... "I just can't forgive that."


**Why Forgiveness Feels Impossible**

Those words have power, don't they? "I just can't forgive that." They feel true. They feel justified. They feel like the only reasonable response to what happened to you.

And maybe they are reasonable. Maybe what happened to you was genuinely terrible. Maybe the person who hurt you doesn't deserve forgiveness. Maybe forgiving them feels like betraying yourself or minimizing what they did.

Maybe you've been told you should forgive, and part of you rebels against that advice. After all, why should you forgive? Why should you be the one to do the work when they're the one who caused the problem? Why should you have to fix what they broke? It doesn't seem fair.

Maybe forgiveness feels like weakness. Like you're letting them off the hook. Like you're saying what they did was okay, when it absolutely wasn't okay.

Maybe you're afraid that if you forgive, you'll become a doormat. That you'll be vulnerable to being hurt again. That people will think you don't value yourself enough to stay angry when someone wrongs you.

## You're Not Alone in This

If any of those thoughts sound familiar, you're not alone. These are the reasons most people can't forgive. These are the walls that keep people stuck for years, sometimes for a lifetime.

Or maybe you've been stuck so long that being angry has become familiar. It's become part of your identity, even if you don't realize it. It's slowly become part of who you are. The person who was wronged. The person who has every right to be upset. The person whose anger proves that what happened mattered.

Whatever your reasons, they make sense. I'm not here to argue with you about whether you should feel the way you feel. You feel how you feel for good reasons.

## Your Anger Makes Sense

Here's what I want you to know... your anger makes sense.

If someone betrayed your trust, your anger is understandable.

If someone hurt you physically or emotionally, of course you're angry.

If someone took something from you that you can't get back, your anger is reasonable.

If someone lied about you or to you, your anger is valid.

Your anger is information. It's telling you that something important to you was damaged. It's telling you that a boundary was crossed. It's telling you that you matter enough to feel upset when you're mistreated. It's giving you information to help you set boundaries so this doesn't happen again. We'll talk more about setting boundaries later in the book.

Your anger is also protection. It's keeping you from immediately jumping back into a situation that might hurt you again. It's giving you energy to defend yourself and figure out what went wrong and what you should do next.

Your anger is validation that something significant happened. It's confirming that what happened was wrong and that you have feelings worth respecting.

I'm not going to tell you that your anger is wrong or that you should just get over it. Your anger serves a purpose, and it makes complete sense given what you've been through.

## But Here's the Thing

And I'm guessing that part of you already knows what I'm about to say next.

Your anger made sense for a time. But that doesn't mean it's serving you well anymore.

There's a difference between anger that protects and motivates you, and anger that imprisons and exhausts you.

There's a difference between anger that validates your worth, and anger that defines your identity.

There's a difference between anger that gives you information about what needs to change, and anger that keeps you stuck in the past.

The question isn't whether your anger is justified. It probably is.

The question isn't whether the person who hurt you deserves forgiveness. They probably don't.

The question is whether you deserve to be free.

Free from carrying this weight every day.

Free from having your peace, or lack of peace, determined by what someone else did or didn't do.

Free from being defined by what happened to you instead of who you choose to become.

Free from the hurt you feel every day in your thoughts and emotions.

## What This Means for You

Your situation is real. Your pain is valid. Your anger makes sense.

But you don't have to stay trapped by what someone else did to you.

You don't have to stay stuck in anger and resentment that steals your peace every single day.

You don't have to choose between forgiving them and valuing yourself.

You don't have to pretend what they did was okay in order to move forward with your life.

What you can choose is to stop letting what they did control what you do with the rest of your life.

What you can choose is to reclaim your peace, your energy, and your future from the grip of past hurts.

What you can choose is to forgive not because they deserve it, but because you deserve it. Because you deserve to be free.

This book isn't going to minimize what happened to you or tell you it wasn't that bad. It was bad. It hurt. It mattered.

This book is going to show you how to heal from it without staying imprisoned by it.

This book is going to help you understand that forgiveness isn't about them... it's about you.

And this book is going to give you practical tools to work through the forgiveness process, even when it feels impossible.

But first, we need to be honest about what staying stuck is costing you.

## 2

# PAYING A HIGH PRICE

Let's be honest about what this anger is actually costing you.

You might not have fully considered the true price you're paying for holding onto what happened to you. It's easy to focus on what the other person did and what they should pay for their actions. But while you've been focused on their debt to you, you're the one who has been paying the price. And it's a really high price.

That person who hurt you? They're living rent-free in your head. And the rent you're paying is higher than you might realize.

### The Physical Cost

Let me show you what I mean. Your body keeps score of unresolved anger in ways you might not even connect to what happened.

Maybe you lie awake at night replaying what they did or what you wish you had said. Your mind won't shut off because it's still trying to solve a problem that can't be solved by thinking about it.

Maybe you wake up tired even when you've slept enough hours. Carrying emotional weight is exhausting, even when you're not consciously thinking about it.

You might notice more headaches than you used to. Tension lives in your shoulders and neck. Your stomach feels unsettled more often. Your jaw aches from clenching it without realizing it.

Maybe you've noticed you get sick more often. Chronic stress weakens your immune system, making you more vulnerable to every cold and flu that goes around.

These aren't just random health problems. Your body is trying to tell you something about the toll this anger is taking.

**The Emotional Cost**

The emotional price might be even higher than the physical one.

How much mental energy do you spend thinking about what happened? Replaying the scene. Imagining what you should have said. Planning what you would say if you saw them again. Rehearsing conversations that will never happen.

How often does thinking about this person or situation ruin an otherwise good day? You're enjoying time with family or friends, and then something reminds you of what happened, and suddenly your mood crashes.

How much harder is it to feel joy about anything when part of your emotional energy is tied up in anger and resentment? It's like trying to run a race with a weight tied to your ankle... you can still move forward, but everything is harder than it should be.

You might find yourself more irritable in general. People who had nothing to do with what happened to you are getting snapped at because your patience is already worn thin from carrying this burden.

Some people notice they feel emotionally numb sometimes. When you're spending so much energy managing anger, there's less capacity for experiencing other emotions fully.

The person who hurt you did their damage once. But you're experiencing it over and over again, every time you think about it.

## The Relational Cost

Unresolved anger doesn't stay contained. It spills over into other relationships, even when you try to keep it separate.

Maybe your family is getting tired of hearing about what happened. They care about you, but they don't know how to help, and bringing it up constantly strains your relationships with people who love you.

You might have become more suspicious of people in general. If one person could betray you like this, how can you trust anyone else? You find yourself looking for red flags in everyone, even people who have given you no reason to doubt them.

Maybe you've pulled back from friendships or avoided making new ones. It feels safer to keep people at a distance than to risk being hurt again.

Your marriage or romantic relationships might be suffering because you're emotionally unavailable. How can you be fully present with someone else when part of your heart is still tied up in anger toward someone who hurt you?

Some people find they've become cynical or bitter in ways that affect how they interact with everyone. The joy and openness you used to bring to relationships has been replaced by guardedness and negativity.

The person who hurt you has managed to damage not just your relationship with them, but your capacity for healthy relationships with everyone else.

## The Spiritual Cost

There's also a spiritual price to pay for carrying unresolved anger, regardless of your religious beliefs.

Maybe you've lost your sense of peace. That deep contentment that comes from feeling secure in who you are and how life works has been replaced by agitation and unrest.

It might be harder to feel grateful for the good things in your life. How can you appreciate what you have when you're focused on what was taken from you?

You might feel disconnected from hope. If this terrible thing could happen to you, what other terrible things might be waiting? Life feels unpredictable and unsafe.

Maybe you struggle with feeling that life is meaningless or unfair. If bad people can do bad things and get away with it, what's the point of trying to be good?

Some people feel spiritually empty, like something essential has been drained out of them. The anger is taking up space that used to be filled with faith, hope, and love.

This spiritual cost might be the highest price of all, because it affects not just how you feel, but how you see the world and your place in it.

## Take Your Own Inventory

Let's get specific about what this is costing you. I want you to think honestly about these questions. You don't have to write anything down unless you want to, but really consider them:

**When you think about the physical impact:** How often do you lose sleep thinking about what happened? What physical symptoms do you experience more often now than before this happened? How has your energy level changed since this occurred?

**When you think about the emotional impact:** How much time each day do you spend thinking about this person or situation? How often does thinking about this ruin an otherwise good day? How has this affected your ability to enjoy other areas of your life?

**When you think about the relational impact:** How has this affected your relationships with family and friends? Have you become more suspicious or guarded with people in general? Are you less available emotionally to the people who care about you?

**When you think about the spiritual impact:** How has this affected your sense of peace and contentment? Has it become harder to feel grateful or hopeful? Do you feel more cynical about life in general?

**And when you think about time and energy:** If you added up all the time you spend thinking about this situation, what could you have accomplished with that time instead? What opportunities for joy, growth, or connection have you missed because you were focused on this?

When you add it all up, what do you notice?

### The Hard Truth About Who's Paying

Here's something that might be difficult to hear... while you're paying this high price every single day, the person who hurt you has probably moved on with their life.

They're not lying awake thinking about you. They're not stressed about what they did. They're not losing sleep or suffering headaches or straining their other relationships because of what happened between you.

They hurt you once, but that hurt keeps repeating. Every time you replay it, every time it resurfaces, every time it controls your day.

Somehow, they ended up living rent-free in your mind. You didn't choose for them to hurt you in the first place. But there are choices you can make about what comes next, the choices that will help you reclaim your mental space.

They took something from you when they hurt you. And this anger is taking even more. It's taking your peace, your joy, your emotional availability, your physical health, your spiritual well-being.

They're still affecting you without even trying anymore.

Here's what I want you to know... You have permission to reclaim your mental space. You don't need anyone's approval to start taking back this power. You don't need their cooperation to begin healing. You have more control over your healing than you might think, and this book will show you how.

### The Question This Raises

Now that you can see what this anger is actually costing you, a question naturally emerges, "Is it worth it?"

Is holding onto this anger worth the price you're paying in sleep, health, relationships, and peace of mind?

Is proving that you're right worth giving up your emotional freedom?

Is keeping them accountable in your mind worth keeping yourself imprisoned?

You have every right to be angry about what they did. But consider this... do you want to keep experiencing the consequences of their actions?

The anger served a purpose when it first happened. It validated that you were wronged. It gave you energy to protect yourself. It motivated you to make necessary changes.

But what purpose is it serving now?

## What This Means

I'm not asking you to pretend what happened didn't matter. It did matter. It was wrong. You deserved better.

I'm asking you to consider whether staying angry is helping you or hurting you at this point.

I'm asking you to think about whether the person who hurt you deserves to continue having this much power over your daily life.

I'm asking you to consider whether you're ready to stop paying such a high price for someone else's bad choices.

Because here's what most people don't realize, you have more control over this situation than you think you do.

You can't control what they did to you. But you can learn to control how much power it has over your present and future.

You can't make them pay the price they should pay for what they did. But you can stop paying the price you've been paying for carrying it.

## What You're Feeling

The cost of staying angry is becoming clear. And I'm guessing right now you're thinking one of two things... either, "Okay, I see the cost, but I still don't know HOW to forgive" or, "Even knowing the cost, I still feel like forgiveness is impossible."

Both responses make sense.

Let's take a look at why you just can't forgive.

## 3

---

# WHY FORGIVENESS FEELS
# IMPOSSIBLE

Even after seeing what anger is costing you... the sleepless nights, the strained relationships, the emotional exhaustion... you're probably still thinking, "Okay, but I STILL just can't forgive what they did."

Good. That means you're taking this seriously.

If forgiveness felt easy right now, I'd be concerned that you weren't taking what happened to you seriously enough. The resistance you feel toward forgiveness isn't a character flaw. It's not evidence that you're petty or vindictive. It's evidence that you're human, and that what happened to you mattered.

But let's look at what's actually behind that resistance. Because understanding why your brain is fighting this idea so hard is the first step toward moving through it.

### Where These Fears Come From

Before we dive into the specific fears you might be experiencing, it helps to understand where they come from.

Some of your resistance to forgiveness comes from messages you learned growing up.

Maybe your family taught you that people who forgive are weak, or that holding grudges is how you protect yourself.

Maybe you learned that anger is how you show love for someone who's been hurt... that if you really cared about your child, you'd never forgive someone who hurt them.

Maybe your culture values honor and revenge over mercy and healing.

Maybe you learned that forgiveness is something you earn through suffering or penance, not something you give freely.

Maybe you've seen forgiveness used as a tool of manipulation... people who claim to forgive but then hold the offense over someone's head forever.

These messages shape how you think about forgiveness without you even realizing it. They make forgiveness feel wrong or dangerous or impossible before you even consider what it might actually mean.

There's also something else at work here... your brain's natural preference for familiar pain over unfamiliar change. Anger is what you know. It's become comfortable, even if it's uncomfortable. It's predictable. You know how to be angry. You've been practicing it.

Forgiveness is unknown territory. You don't know who you'll be without this anger. You don't know how you'll feel. Your brain interprets unfamiliar as dangerous, even when familiar is painful.

With that in mind, let's look at the specific fears that might be keeping you stuck.

**Fear #1: They'll Get Off Without Consequences**

Maybe your biggest fear about forgiveness is that it lets them off the hook.

If you forgive them, they win. They hurt you and faced no real consequences for their actions. They got to do damage to your life and then walk away free while you're the one who has to do all the work to heal from it.

That feels fundamentally unfair, doesn't it?

You want them to acknowledge what they did. You want them to understand how much they hurt you. You want them to experience consequence that matches the damage they caused. You want justice.

And anger feels like the only way to ensure they don't just get away with it. Your anger feels like evidence that what they did was wrong. It feels like the only consequence they're facing. It feels like the only tool you have to hold them accountable.

If you let go of the anger, who's going to hold them accountable? Who's going to remember what they did? Who's going to make sure they pay some kind of price?

This fear runs deep because it touches something fundamental, the human need for justice. When someone does wrong, there should be consequences. When someone causes harm, there should be accountability. That's how the world is supposed to work.

And when the world doesn't work that way... when someone hurts you and faces no real consequences... it feels like a violation of the moral order of things. Your anger becomes the only thing standing between what happened and complete injustice.

I understand that. The desire for justice isn't wrong. The sense that consequences matter isn't misplaced. What happened to you shouldn't just be swept under the rug and forgotten.

But here's the hard truth you need to hear... your anger isn't actually creating consequences for them. It's creating consequences for you.

They're not lying awake at night because you're angry with them. They're not stressed or suffering because you refuse to forgive them. Your anger isn't teaching them a lesson or making them think twice about their choices.

Your anger is only punishing one person... you.

Think about it. If your anger were an effective tool for holding them accountable, wouldn't they be feeling it by now? Wouldn't they be suffering under the weight of your unforgiveness?

The truth is, accountability and consequences aren't your responsibility to deliver through your anger. You're trying to use anger as a tool it was never designed to be. It's like trying to use a hammer to cut wood... you can keep hitting the board, but it's not going to work, and you're going to exhaust yourself trying.

Justice matters. But your anger isn't justice. It's just you carrying the weight of what they should be carrying.

**Fear #2: Forgiveness Equals Weakness**

Maybe you've been taught that anger shows strength and self-respect while forgiveness shows weakness.

Strong people stand up for themselves. They don't let others walk all over them. They fight back when they're wronged. They show they have backbone by refusing to forgive people who hurt them.

Forgiveness feels like rolling over and playing dead. It feels like saying, "It's okay, you can treat me however you want." It feels like announcing to the world that you don't value yourself enough to stay mad when someone wrongs you.

You might be afraid that if you forgive, people will see you as a pushover. They'll think you're naive or that you don't have enough self-respect to defend yourself.

Maybe you've seen people who forgive too quickly or too easily, and they seem to get hurt over and over again because they don't protect themselves.

Maybe you've been taught that anger is how you show the world you matter. That getting mad proves you have standards. That staying mad proves you have dignity.

Your brain likes this narrative because it's familiar. It's what you've practiced. Staying angry requires no growth, no change, no difficult choices. It's actually the path of least resistance emotionally.

But consider this... which really takes more strength, staying angry or choosing to let go?

Think about Gary Hagen from the introduction. Did he look weak when he chose to meet with his son's killer? Or did that take more courage than staying angry would have? The families who forgave murder aren't weak, they're some of the strongest people you'll ever encounter.

Choosing forgiveness when you have every right to stay angry? That takes real strength. That takes courage. That takes someone who is secure enough in their own worth that they don't need other people's suffering to validate their value.

You might be surprised to discover that the people you admire most for their strength are often people who chose to let go rather than hold on.

### Fear #3: Some Things Are Actually Unforgivable

Maybe you believe that what happened to you falls into the category of truly unforgivable offenses.

Some things are just too big, too harmful, too evil to forgive. Murder. Abuse. Betrayal. Rape. Abandonment. Cruelty to children. Some lines, once crossed, can never be uncrossed.

You might accept that forgiveness is possible for smaller offenses... someone who's rude to you, or who forgets your birthday, or who says something thoughtless. But what happened to you isn't small. It's not the kind of thing you can just "get over."

The damage was too great. The trust was too completely broken. The harm was too intentional. Some things simply cannot and should not be forgiven.

I'm not going to try to convince you that what happened to you wasn't that bad. It was bad. The harm was real. The damage matters. And I'm not going to minimize that by comparing suffering... your pain is your pain, and it's real.

I also understand why your brain wants to put some offenses in the "unforgivable" category. It's a way of honoring the seriousness of what happened. It's a way of saying "this mattered." It's a way of maintaining the moral order... some things are so wrong that they're beyond forgiveness.

What I am going to suggest is this... the "unforgivable" category might not actually be about the severity of what happened. It might be about something else entirely.

The families in our introduction forgave murder. Not because murder isn't serious. They didn't minimize what happened or pretend it wasn't that bad.

They discovered something important... forgiveness wasn't about whether the offense deserved to be forgiven. It was about whether they deserved to be free.

Forgiveness isn't a statement about how bad what they did was. It's a statement about how good your life can be when you're not controlled by what they did.

The question isn't whether what they did is forgivable. The question is whether you want to stay chained to it for the rest of your life.

### Fear #4: They Have to Ask for It First

Maybe you believe that forgiveness isn't something you can offer until it's something they've requested.

They should come to you. They should acknowledge what they did. They should apologize sincerely and ask for your forgiveness. Then, maybe, you can consider whether to give it.

Until they do that, forgiveness isn't even on the table. You're not about to hand them something they haven't even bothered to ask for.

This makes logical sense. Why should you do all the emotional work of forgiving someone who isn't even sorry for what they did? Why should you release them from a debt they haven't even acknowledged owing?

Your brain likes this because it feels like maintaining control. They started this situation by hurting you. The least they can do is take the first step toward resolution by apologizing.

But think about what this belief is actually doing to you.

It means your healing is dependent on their choices. Your peace is controlled by their actions. Your freedom is held hostage by someone who has already proven they don't have your best interests at heart.

You're essentially saying, "I'll be okay as soon as the person who hurt me decides to help me be okay." That gives them incredible power over your life... power they've already misused once.

What if they never apologize? What if they never even realize they hurt you? What if they're incapable of genuine remorse? What if they're dead?

Does that mean you never get to heal? Does that mean you never get to be free? Does that mean what they did gets to control you for the rest of your life?

## Fear #5: I'll Be Vulnerable to Being Hurt Again

Underneath all these other fears is often one deeper fear... that if you forgive, you'll be vulnerable to being hurt again.

Anger feels like armor. It feels like protection. It feels like insurance against future pain.

If you stay angry, you won't trust them again. You won't let your guard down. You won't give them another opportunity to hurt you. Your anger is a wall that keeps them, and the pain they caused, at a safe distance.

If you forgive, you might soften. You might let them back in. You might forget how much they're capable of hurting you. You might become naive again, vulnerable again, the person who got hurt in the first place.

This fear makes complete sense. You've been hurt before. Your brain is trying to prevent that from happening again. Anger feels like the best defense mechanism you have.

Your brain prefers this familiar protection, even if it's painful, because the alternative... being vulnerable again... feels dangerous.

But this fear is based on a misunderstanding of what forgiveness actually means.

Forgiveness doesn't mean trusting someone who's proven themselves untrustworthy. It doesn't mean giving someone who hurt you another chance to hurt you. It doesn't mean pretending what they did wasn't serious or that they're not capable of doing it again.

You can forgive someone and still protect yourself from them. You can release your anger and still maintain healthy boundaries. You can choose freedom from resentment without choosing vulnerability to future harm.

The armor you think is protecting you has actually become a prison. It's not just keeping them out... it's keeping you locked in.

## What This All Adds Up To

All of these fears and concerns about forgiveness are understandable. They make sense given what you've experienced and what you've been taught.

Also, you've invested a lot in being right about this situation. You've spent time and energy building your case against this person. You've told other people what they did. You've thought through all the ways they were wrong and you were wronged.

Forgiveness might feel like admitting you were wrong to be angry, or that you wasted all that time and energy, or that your feelings didn't matter as much as you thought they did.

But forgiveness isn't about admitting you were wrong to be angry. It's about choosing to be free even though you were right to be angry.

Your resistance isn't evidence that you're a bad person. It's evidence that you're trying to protect yourself, maintain your dignity, and ensure that what happened to you matters.

The problem is that your protection has become a prison. Your attempt to maintain dignity has become a source of suffering. Your effort to make your pain matter has become a way of giving that pain more power over your life.

Understanding why forgiveness feels impossible is the first step toward discovering that it might actually be possible after all.

Now, let's look at the important role anger plays.

## 4

---

# FROM WALLS TO BOUNDARIES

After being hurt, you did what any reasonable person would do... you built walls to protect yourself.

Those walls made perfect sense at the time. They kept you safe. They gave you space to process what happened. They prevented you from immediately jumping back into a situation that might hurt you again.

But somewhere along the way, those protective walls became something else entirely.

They became your prison.

### Why You Built Walls

Let's be clear about something, building walls after being hurt isn't a character flaw. It's a survival response.

When someone betrays your trust, when someone wounds you deeply, when someone takes advantage of your vulnerability... your instinct is to protect yourself from that ever happening again.

So you build walls.

Maybe your wall looks like refusing to trust anyone. If you don't trust people, they can't betray you.

Maybe your wall looks like keeping everyone at arm's length emotionally. If you don't let people get close, they can't hurt you.

Maybe your wall looks like staying angry. If you stay mad at the person who hurt you, you won't soften toward them and become vulnerable again.

Maybe your wall looks like cynicism about relationships in general. If you expect everyone to disappoint you, you won't be surprised when they do.

These walls served a purpose when you first built them. They gave you breathing room. They protected you from additional pain while you were still raw and wounded. They created a safe space where you could begin to process what happened.

This was smart. This was healthy. This was exactly what you needed at that moment.

The problem is that walls that were meant to be temporary often become permanent. Protection that was necessary for a season becomes a prison for a lifetime.


## How Walls Become Prisons

Here's the thing about walls, they're not selective. They don't just keep out the bad. They keep out everything.

When you build a wall to keep out people who might hurt you, that same wall keeps out people who might love you well.

When you build a wall to protect yourself from betrayal, that same wall prevents you from experiencing genuine connection.

When you build a wall to ensure you're never vulnerable again, that same wall guarantees you'll never be truly known.

Walls are binary. You're either inside or you're outside. Everyone gets the same treatment... total access or total exclusion. There's no nuance, no discernment, no wisdom in how walls operate.

And walls require constant maintenance.

You have to stay vigilant. You have to keep reinforcing them. You have to watch for any sign that someone might be trying to get through. You have to patrol the perimeter constantly, looking for threats.

That's exhausting.

Think about all the energy you spend maintaining your walls. The mental effort of staying guarded. The emotional work of keeping people at a distance. The relational cost of treating everyone as a potential threat.

You built the walls to protect yourself, but now you're trapped behind them. The very thing that was supposed to give you safety has stolen your freedom.

You're isolated. You're alone. You're safe from being hurt again, perhaps. But you're also cut off from joy, from connection, from the very things that make life worth living.

The walls aren't protecting you anymore. They're imprisoning you.


**What Boundaries Look Like**

There's a better way to protect yourself. It's called boundaries.

Boundaries are completely different from walls.

Walls say, "No one gets in. Everyone is a threat. I'm shutting down completely."

Boundaries say, "I'm going to be thoughtful about who gets access to different parts of my life. I'm going to make wise decisions about trust. I'm going to protect myself without isolating myself."

Here's how boundaries work...

**Boundaries are discerning.** They don't treat everyone the same. They recognize that some people have earned trust and some people haven't. They allow you to have different levels of connection with different people based on their trustworthiness.

**Boundaries are flexible.** They can adjust based on the situation and the person. Your boundary with someone who has proven themselves trustworthy looks different from your boundary with someone who has shown themselves to be unsafe.

**Boundaries are selective.** They let good things in while keeping harmful things out. They're like a filter, not a fortress. They allow for connection while maintaining protection.

**Boundaries require wisdom.** Unlike walls, which are automatic and absolute, boundaries require you to think, to assess, to make judgments about people and situations. They require maturity.

A boundary might sound like:

• "I'll have a relationship with you, but I won't share personal information until you've proven trustworthy."

• "I'll forgive what you did, but I won't put myself in a position where you could do it again."

• "I'll be friendly with you, but I won't be close friends until I see consistent evidence that you've changed."

• "I'll co-parent with you effectively, but I won't discuss anything beyond the children's needs."

Boundaries allow you to engage with life and relationships without being naive or reckless. They allow you to learn from your past without being controlled by it. They allow you to be wise without being closed off.

Walls keep you frozen in time, stuck at the moment when you were hurt. Boundaries allow you to grow, to learn, to become someone who can navigate relationships with wisdom and discernment.

## The Choice You Face

Here's what I need you to understand, you're going to have to choose to tear down the walls and learn to build boundaries instead.

No one can make this choice for you.

Your friends can encourage you. Your counselor can guide you. This book can give you tools and understanding. But the fundamental choice to move from walls to boundaries? That has to come from you.

This is hard work. It requires something from you that hiding behind walls doesn't require.

Walls are simple. They're binary. They don't require wisdom or discernment or maturity. They just require you to shut down and shut everyone out.

Boundaries are complex. They require you to think. To assess. To make judgment calls about people and situations. They require you to become someone who can protect themselves without isolating themselves.

But here's the truth, you can't stay behind your walls and heal. You can't stay isolated and find peace. You can't keep everyone out and still experience the fullness of life.

The walls that protected you initially are now preventing your healing.

If you want to move forward, if you want to be free, if you want to reclaim your life from what happened to you, you're going to have to make this choice.

You're going to have to be willing to tear down the walls and do the harder work of building healthy boundaries.

This is the work that transforms you from someone who was hurt into someone who is moving forward.

## Why This Changes Everything

Here's why this choice matters so much... you can't move forward from behind a wall.

When you're walled off, everything is frozen. The hurt is frozen. The anger is frozen. The relationship, or the memory of the relationship, is frozen in that moment of betrayal.

Nothing can move. Nothing can change. Nothing can heal.

Walls preserve everything exactly as it was. They keep the offense fresh, the anger alive, the pain immediate. That's what walls do... they freeze time at the moment of maximum hurt.

But when you learn to build boundaries instead of walls, something shifts.

Boundaries allow you to acknowledge what happened without being consumed by it. They allow you to protect yourself without imprisoning yourself. They allow you to move forward without pretending the past didn't happen.

Boundaries give you the safety you need to actually process what happened and let it go.

Think about it this way... when you're behind a wall, you can't let go of the anger because the anger IS the wall. Your resentment is what keeps everyone out. Your bitterness is your protection. If you forgave, you'd lose your defenses, and that feels terrifying.

But when you have healthy boundaries, you don't need anger for protection anymore. You have wisdom. You have discernment. You have the ability to protect yourself while still being open to life and relationships.

You can forgive the person who hurt you because you're no longer depending on your anger toward them to keep you safe. Your boundaries keep you safe. Your wisdom keeps you safe.

Freedom becomes possible when you realize you can let go of the anger and forgive without becoming vulnerable to being hurt in the same way again.

This is the fundamental choice that makes everything else in this book possible. You have to choose to move from walls to boundaries. You have to choose to become someone who can navigate relationships with wisdom rather than fear.

You're not choosing to be naive again. You're not choosing to pretend what happened didn't hurt. You're not choosing to trust people who haven't earned it.

You're choosing to be wise. You're choosing to protect yourself in a way that actually works without destroying your capacity for joy and connection.

### What This Looks Like

So what does it actually look like to tear down walls and build boundaries?

It starts with recognizing that not everyone deserves the same level of access to your life. Some people have earned deep trust. Some people have earned surface-level friendliness. Some people have earned nothing but polite distance.

It means learning to assess people based on their actual behavior, not on your fear of being hurt. It means giving people appropriate levels of trust and adjusting that trust based on how they handle it.

It means being willing to be hurt again... not by being reckless or naive... but by being brave enough to stay open to life and relationships even knowing that hurt is possible.

It means developing wisdom about red flags, about patterns of behavior, about what trustworthiness actually looks like.

It means being able to say things like:

• "I notice you did X, and that concerns me. I'm going to need to see Y before I can trust you with Z."

• "I've forgiven what happened, but I'm not comfortable with that level of closeness anymore."

• "I can have a cordial relationship with you, but I won't be sharing personal information."

• "I'm willing to try again, but these are the boundaries I need in place for that to work."

Building boundaries is harder than hiding behind walls. It requires more from you. It requires you to think, to feel, to assess, to make difficult decisions.

But it's also what sets you free.


**The Path Forward**

Right now, you're standing at a crossroads.

Behind you are the walls you've built for protection. They've kept you safe, but they've also kept you stuck. They've protected you from additional hurt, but they've also prevented your healing.

In front of you is the harder path of tearing down those walls and learning to build healthy boundaries instead. It's the path of growth, of wisdom, of actually dealing with what happened instead of just defending against it.

You have to choose which path you're going to take.

If you choose to stay behind your walls, you'll stay safe from some things, but you'll also stay imprisoned. You'll avoid some pain, but you'll also miss out on healing, on growth, on the possibility of actually being free.

If you choose to tear down the walls and build boundaries, you're choosing the harder path. But you're also choosing the path that leads to actual freedom. To real healing. To the possibility of living fully again without being controlled by what happened to you.

I can't make this choice for you. No one can.

But I can tell you this... choosing boundaries over walls is what makes it possible to get your life back. It's what creates the conditions for healing. It's what allows you to move from being someone who was hurt to being someone who is wise.

When you're ready to make that choice, the rest of this book will show you how.

Now that you understand the choice you're facing, let's be clear about what forgiveness actually means... and what it doesn't mean.

## 5

# WHAT FORGIVENESS IS AND ISN'T

Before you can choose forgiveness, you need to know what you're actually choosing.

Most people resist forgiveness because they're afraid of the wrong thing. They think forgiveness means something it doesn't mean. They imagine it requires something it doesn't require. They worry it will cost them something it won't cost them.

Let's clear up these misconceptions so you can make an informed decision about whether forgiveness is something you want to pursue.

### What Forgiveness Is NOT

Let's start by clarifying what forgiveness isn't.

### Forgiveness Is Not Forgetting

"Forgive and forget" might be a popular saying, but it's terrible advice.

Forgetting what happened would be dangerous. Your memory of what happened serves an important purpose... it protects you from being hurt in the same way again. It reminds you what red flags to watch for. It helps you make wiser decisions about who to trust and how much to trust them.

If someone stole money from you, forgetting that happened would make you vulnerable to being robbed by the same person again. If someone betrayed your confidence, forgetting that betrayal would leave you defenseless against future manipulation.

Forgiveness doesn't erase your memory. It changes how that memory affects you.

When you forgive, you still remember what happened, but the memory no longer controls your emotional state. You can think about what they did without being consumed by anger. You can remember the betrayal without being overwhelmed by bitterness.

Your memory becomes information instead of ammunition. It becomes wisdom instead of a weapon.

### Forgiveness Is Not Excusing Their Behavior

Forgiveness doesn't make what they did okay. It doesn't minimize the damage they caused. It doesn't pretend their actions were acceptable or understandable or justified.

You can forgive someone and still believe they were completely wrong. You can release your anger toward them while maintaining that their behavior was inexcusable.

Forgiveness is not about their behavior. It's about your freedom.

When you forgive, you're not saying, "What you did was fine." You're saying, "What you did was wrong, and I'm choosing not to let it control my life anymore."

## Forgiveness Is Not Letting Them Off the Hook

Forgiveness doesn't make someone immune from consequences. It doesn't prevent justice from being served. It doesn't mean they shouldn't face legal, professional, or social repercussions for their actions.

If someone committed a crime against you, forgiving them doesn't mean you shouldn't press charges. If someone violated professional ethics, forgiving them doesn't mean you shouldn't report them. If someone harmed others, forgiving them doesn't mean you shouldn't warn those people.

You are not their judge, their jury, or their parole officer. Natural consequences for their actions can still occur whether you forgive them or not.

Your forgiveness is about your internal peace, not their external circumstances.


## Forgiveness Is Not Reconciliation

This might be the most important distinction to understand... forgiveness and reconciliation are two completely different things.

Forgiveness is something you do by yourself, for yourself. It's an internal process that doesn't require the other person's participation, cooperation, or even awareness.

Reconciliation is the restoration of a relationship. It requires both people to want the relationship restored and both people to do the work necessary to rebuild trust.

You can forgive someone and never speak to them again. You can release your anger toward them and still choose not to have them in your life. You can find peace about what happened and still maintain complete distance from the person who hurt you.

Forgiveness opens the door to the possibility of reconciliation, but it doesn't require you to walk through that door. Whether or not to reconcile is a separate decision that requires careful thought, wise counsel, and evidence of real change from the other person.

## Forgiveness Is Not Becoming a Doormat

Forgiveness doesn't mean accepting future mistreatment. It doesn't mean lowering your standards or weakening your boundaries. It doesn't mean becoming naive about people's capacity to hurt you.

You can forgive someone and still refuse to give them another opportunity to hurt you. You can release resentment toward them and still protect yourself from them. You can choose peace about the past and still maintain firm boundaries for the future.

Actually, forgiveness often makes you stronger, not weaker. When you're no longer controlled by anger and resentment, you can think more clearly about what healthy boundaries look like. When you're not consumed by what someone did to you, you have more energy to protect yourself from future harm.

## Forgiveness Is Not Dependent on Their Apology

You don't have to wait for them to apologize before you can forgive them. You don't need their remorse, their acknowledgment, or their cooperation to find your own healing.

Waiting for their apology means your healing is dependent on their choices. Your peace is controlled by their actions. Your freedom is held hostage by someone who has already proven they don't have your best interests at heart.

What if they never apologize? What if they never realize they hurt you? What if they're incapable of genuine remorse? What if they're dead?

Does that mean you never get to heal? Does that mean you stay trapped forever?

Forgiveness is something you do for yourself, regardless of what they do or don't do.

## Forgiveness Is Not a One-Time Decision

Forgiveness is often a process, not an event. You might have to choose it repeatedly, especially for significant hurts.

You might forgive someone on Monday and find yourself angry again on Tuesday. That doesn't mean you failed at forgiveness. That means you're human, and healing takes time.

You might think you've completely forgiven someone, only to have the anger resurface when you see them or when something reminds you of what they did. That's normal. That's part of the process.

Forgiveness is like physical therapy after an injury. You don't do it once and expect to be completely healed. You do it consistently, over time, until you regain full function.

## Forgiveness Is Not Pretending to Be Over It

Fake forgiveness helps no one. Pretending you're fine when you're not fine doesn't lead to real healing. Saying you forgive someone when you're still consumed with anger toward them is just denial with religious language.

It's okay to still feel hurt while you're working toward forgiveness. It's okay to admit that you're struggling to let go. It's okay to say, "I want to forgive, but I'm not there yet."

Honest struggle is better than false peace. Authentic process is better than pretended completion.

Real forgiveness takes time, and it's okay to be honest about where you are in that process.

## What Forgiveness IS

Now that we've cleared up what forgiveness isn't, let's talk about what it actually is.

### Forgiveness Is a Banking Term

At its core, forgiveness is a financial concept. When you forgive a debt, you cancel what someone owes you. You release them from their obligation to pay you back.

When someone hurts you, they create a debt. They owe you an apology, an explanation, restitution, or some form of payment for the damage they caused.

When you forgive them, you're canceling that debt. You're saying, "My peace is worth more than trying to collect what you owe me."

This doesn't mean what they did was free. It cost you something... your trust, your security, your peace of mind. But you're choosing to absorb that cost rather than continuing to try to collect a payment from them... a payment that you may never get.

### Forgiveness Is a Conscious Choice

Forgiveness is not a feeling that happens to you. It's a decision you make.

You don't wait to feel forgiving before you choose to forgive. You choose to forgive, and the feelings eventually follow.

This is actually encouraging news. It means forgiveness doesn't depend on your emotions, which can be unpredictable and uncontrollable. It depends on your will, which you have authority over.

You can choose to forgive someone even when you don't feel like it. You can decide to cancel their debt even when your emotions are still demanding payment.

### Forgiveness Is About Your Freedom

The primary beneficiary of forgiveness is not the person who hurt you. It's you.

When you forgive, you're not doing them a favor. You're doing yourself a favor. You're choosing your own freedom over your own bondage.

You're choosing to stop carrying their debt. You're choosing to stop letting what they did control your daily emotional experience. You're choosing to reclaim the mental and emotional energy you've been spending on resenting them.

Forgiveness is the ultimate act of self-care.

### Forgiveness Is Possible Regardless of Their Response

Your ability to forgive doesn't depend on their cooperation. They don't have to participate in your healing process.

They can remain unrepentant, and you can still forgive them. They can refuse to acknowledge what they did, and you can still find peace about it. They can continue to be the same person who hurt you, and you can still choose freedom from resentment toward them.

Your forgiveness is about your choices, not theirs.

### Forgiveness Is Compatible with Justice

Forgiving someone doesn't prevent justice from being served. You can forgive someone and still support appropriate consequences for their actions.

You can forgive someone who stole from you and still expect them to make restitution. You can forgive someone who committed a crime and still testify at their trial. You can forgive someone who hurt others and still protect those people from future harm.

Justice and forgiveness serve different purposes. Justice addresses the wrong that was done. Forgiveness addresses the ongoing damage that holding onto anger does to you.

## Forgiveness Is Compatible with Boundaries

You can forgive someone and still protect yourself from them. You can release resentment toward them and still refuse to trust them.

Forgiveness deals with the past. Boundaries deal with the future.

You can forgive what they did and still decide you don't want them in your life. You can find peace about what happened and still choose not to give them another opportunity to hurt you.

Healthy boundaries after forgiveness aren't about punishing them. They're about protecting yourself.

The boundaries you learned to build in the last chapter? Those are what make forgiveness safe. You can let go of the anger because you're no longer depending on that anger for protection. Your boundaries protect you now.

## Why This Matters

Understanding what forgiveness actually means removes most of the barriers that keep people from choosing it.

You don't have to worry about becoming vulnerable to future harm. You can forgive and still protect yourself with healthy boundaries.

You don't have to worry about excusing their behavior. You can forgive and still believe they were wrong.

You don't have to worry about letting them off the hook. You can forgive and still support appropriate consequences.

You don't have to worry about being forced back into a relationship with someone unsafe. You can forgive and still maintain distance.

You don't have to wait for them to cooperate with your healing. You can forgive regardless of what they do.

Forgiveness is actually much safer than most people think it is. It's also much more powerful.

When you understand that forgiveness is primarily about your freedom, not their benefit, it becomes much more appealing.

When you realize that forgiveness doesn't require you to compromise your safety or your values, it becomes much less frightening.

When you see that forgiveness is something you can choose regardless of their response, it becomes much more possible.

**The Key Questions**

Now that you understand what forgiveness actually means, the questions become...

Do you want to be free?

Do you want to stop carrying the weight of what they did to you?

Do you want to reclaim the mental and emotional energy you've been spending on resentment?

Do you want to stop letting what they did control your daily experience?

Do you want to stop trying to collect payment from someone who may never pay?

If the answer is yes, then forgiveness might be exactly what you need.

You've already made the choice to tear down walls and build boundaries. You've already chosen the path of wisdom and growth.

Now it's time to understand the process of actually working through forgiveness. That's where we'll turn our attention next.

# 6

# THE FOUR STEPS OF THE FORGIVENESS PROCESS

Now that we understand what forgiveness is and what it isn't, let's dig into the steps people go through as they process forgiveness.

We'll explore together why each step matters and see where people commonly get stuck in the process.

For now, just focus on understanding the forgiveness process itself.

Don't get stressed when you read through it. It's completely normal to feel overwhelmed as you start learning how to get from "I just can't forgive that" to actually working through forgiveness.

We'll work through it together. You will find your path to move through the forgiveness process.

Even if you feel completely stuck at one of these steps right now, you'll find your way to get moving forward when we get to part two of this book.

For now, it's just important to understand the steps. Don't worry too much about how you're going to get through all of them yet.

**Step One: Awareness**

There's a moment in time when you realize that someone has done something to offend or hurt you. Until that moment, you weren't aware.

Now, you're painfully aware.

Maybe you feel hurt. Maybe you feel foolish for letting someone take advantage of you. Maybe you feel betrayed. Maybe you feel blindsided.

However you felt in that moment, everything changed when you realized what had been done to you.

What can add to the shock is how you discover the offense. Were you stunned when you caught the person in the act? Did someone else tell you what happened? Did the pieces of the puzzle slowly come together until it became obvious what had happened?

At first, it may not even seem real.

You're shocked. Your mind is spinning. It seems so surreal.

You begin to question, "Did this really happen?"

Or you think, "How could this happen to me?"

Sometimes this phase lasts just moments. Sometimes it lasts days or even weeks. You might find yourself in a fog, going through the motions of your day while your mind keeps circling back to what happened.

Your worldview is shaken. Your map of how things should be suddenly doesn't line up with what has happened. You start replaying the scene over and over in your mind, trying to make sense of it.

You may have had a physical response. Maybe you felt like you had been punched in the stomach. Or you had that sinking feeling in your chest. Perhaps you broke out in hives or started shaking. Some people describe feeling nauseous or unable to eat. Others can't sleep, lying awake replaying everything.

This step is important because it makes you aware of something that has happened. And that you need to sort it out.

Maybe the person did something to you on purpose. Maybe the person wasn't even aware they did anything to you at all. Right now, you may not know. You may just know something happened, and it hurt.

This awareness step usually goes fast, though it might not feel fast while you're in it. Your emotions quickly move from shock or disbelief to the emotion that gets its own step in the forgiveness process.

Anger.

## Step Two: Anger

Once you become aware that something happened, it's common to move quickly to feeling angry.

Then, normally, the steps of the forgiveness process come to a grinding halt.

Anger is where you will likely stay for a long time. Perhaps for a lifetime. Unless you learn how to make forgiveness a part of your life.

Whatever happened, you feel angry. Maybe rightfully so. Maybe from habit. But the anger is real, and it's powerful.

Now, you might be surprised by what I'm about to say, **this step is important because anger can actually serve you.**

Let me explain what I mean.

## The Good Side of Anger

Anger can be a signal that something isn't right and needs to be handled. Anger can protect you. Anger can be a source of information. Anger can motivate you.

If the person did something on purpose... or even inadvertently... anger is a validation that what happened was wrong. You have feelings. You and your feelings matter. You have boundaries. You have enough self-respect to not accept being mistreated.

Anger can be a protection mechanism. It can give you energy to protect yourself or your child. Anger can be a fence, preventing you from immediately returning to a harmful situation. That's good. That's healthy. That fence is keeping you safe while you figure things out.

Anger can give you important information. Anger has a way of revealing your boundaries and what you care about. It shows you where you feel powerless. It highlights what matters most to you.

Anger can motivate you to take appropriate action... to set and protect boundaries, and to give you the strength to make necessary changes. It can give you the energy to leave the rut you've been stuck in.

Maybe you didn't realize anger could be good and useful.

Your anger serves a purpose. It wakes you up. It protects you. It shows you what matters.

But here's where things get complicated.


## When Anger Stops Serving You

The danger of this step of the forgiveness process is that anger can become a habit.

Anger can feel good. When you're angry, the focus is on the other person and not on what you may need to work on.

It can become a shortcut to remove any responsibility from you and to place the responsibility for action fully on the other person. This can lead you to believe that since you've done nothing wrong, you shouldn't have to do any work to resolve the issue.

But here's the uncomfortable truth, even if the other person caused the offense... and you are rightfully angry... your anger may point to work you need to do on yourself.

Another negative aspect of anger is that hurt feelings can become a powerful tool to manipulate others. Sometimes anger is a result of being overly sensitive rather than a result of a genuine offense. I'm not saying that's what's happening with you. I'm just saying it's important to be honest with ourselves about our anger.

It's important to realize there can be a dark side to anger.

The goal is to use your anger for good... for information, protection, and motivation... rather than as a place to set up permanent residence.

Because that's what happens to most people. They move into anger, and never leave.

### Step Three: A High Price to Pay

You may have never moved to step three of the forgiveness process. It's very common to stay stuck on step two, in your anger.

It may have never come to mind that you're paying a high price to stay in your anger.

Let me show you what I mean.

### How Anger Served You at First

When you initially realized what happened, your anger gave you important information, protection, and motivation.

You played the scenario over and over in your memory. You thought about how you could have done things differently. You considered what red flags you should be looking for.

At some level, you're thinking that you can't let this happen again.

You can feel your anger pushing you to sort out what you need to do differently.

There is real value in this anger-driven thought process.

Your anger woke you up to a situation that went against your values or crossed your boundaries. It brought important information to the front of your mind. It brought focus to something you missed. Something that didn't match your current understanding of how the world works.

Having something unexpected happen made you feel like you didn't know what to do next. So you put up a fence to protect yourself or your child. Putting up a fence gave you time to adjust your perception of reality. It protects you from jumping back into a dangerous situation.

Changing can be hard to do, even when it's in our best interest. Our default can tend to be towards staying stuck. Your anger woke up something inside of you that motivated you to change.

That leads us to the real purpose of memory.


## The Real Purpose of Memory

Many people think memory is to remember that fun vacation or happy times with a friend. There's certainly nothing wrong with those memories, but that's not the main purpose of memory.

The primary purpose of memory is to remember the things that happened that you didn't expect.

Think about it this way, when life goes exactly as you predicted you don't dwell on it. You don't replay those moments over and over. But when something catches you off guard? When reality doesn't match what you thought would happen? That's what sticks in your memory.

You thought the world worked one way, but you were surprised. You thought you had a mutual understanding with someone, but instead you got hurt or betrayed.

That's what memory does. It brings that unexpected event back to your mind... not to torture you, but to give you the nudge to evaluate and adjust your understanding.

Memory is there to help you learn. To help you see where your map of reality was wrong, so you can redraw it more accurately.

It's pushing you to make important changes... to see the red flags you missed, to understand the patterns you didn't recognize, and to adjust your expectations and boundaries.

Here's what most people don't understand, **once you've learned the lesson and made the changes, the memory's job is done.**

The memory was only there to remind you to remap your perspective to match an unexpected reality.

Once you've done that, the memory no longer serves a purpose.

Anger is no longer needed.

You've integrated that previously unknown reality into your personal map of how the world works. You've learned what you needed to learn. You've made the changes you needed to make.

You can take down the fence and start moving forward again.

You got the value you needed from the anger and the memory of the situation.

It's time to move on.

However, many don't move on.


## What Happens When You Stay

Many people linger in replaying the memories, stoking the fire of their anger, keeping their anger smoldering.

It's understandable why people get stuck here...

Anger can feel good.

It keeps the focus on the other person.

It can be used to justify your choices and actions.

And here's what happens... you start replacing that protective fence with a brick wall, thinking to yourself, "That's never going to happen to me again!"

What was meant to be a fence to protect you from immediately jumping back into a dangerous situation is becoming a fortress.

Your fortress becomes your isolation.

You hang onto that anger.

Because it's what you know.

It becomes comfortable.

It keeps the problem "out there," somewhere else.

Your anger may become part of your identity.

You think to yourself, "I'm the person who was wronged."

You may put yourself on the side of good and the person who offended you on the side of bad.

What they did is living rent-free in your head.

But they've already moved on.

Maybe because that was their plan all along, or because they never even realized they had offended you.

**The Real Cost**

You're stuck in the past. Isolated. Angry.

You are paying an incredibly high price.

The person who offended you isn't.

You've been suffering. They aren't.

Maybe your anger has completely taken over your life while they're living theirs freely.

Here's what you may not have realized, **you don't need an impenetrable fortress.**

Because you made the changes and remapped your perspective, that situation won't ever happen to you again... at least not in the same way.

You don't need an impenetrable fortress to protect you because your protection has been integrated into who you are.

You've used your anger and memories to develop healthy boundaries, and now you know how to effectively protect yourself.

You're wiser.

You know how to prevent that situation or deal with that kind of person in the future.

Because you did the work.

The fence did its job. The anger served its purpose. The memory taught you what you needed to learn.

Now it's time to let the anger and the memory go.

## Step Four: Choosing Forgiveness

At this point, you might be thinking, "I can see how hanging onto my anger leaves me paying a high price."

Maybe you're not happy that you're the one who has to do the work, but you can see that building healthy boundaries is a good thing.

You can see that you don't want to keep paying the high price of staying angry.

However, we haven't talked about how your work on building healthy boundaries relates to forgiveness.

There's one more piece of unfinished business you need to work through at this point.

## The Emotional Baggage That Remains

You probably still have an emotional response when you think about that person and how they offended you.

You're still collecting emotional baggage, and all that extra baggage just keeps stacking up.

The old offenses still have power over you, just in a different way.

Your work to integrate healthy boundaries? That protects you going forward. That's excellent. That's growth. That's wisdom.

But even with great boundaries in place, you're still emotionally tied to the past. You're still carrying around baggage that needs to be set down.

Unforgiveness can keep you connected to people, situations, memories, and emotions that you want to be free from.

**Forgiveness frees you from the past.**

This step is important because you still need to drain the emotion from your memory of the offense.

Choosing to forgive is what takes the emotional sting out of that memory. It prevents that memory from triggering an emotional response in other situations and relationships.

It's the difference between keeping a wound open for the rest of your life... always wondering when it will get infected and painful... and treating the wound so it heals completely.

The scar might remain. You'll remember what happened. But it won't hurt anymore. It won't control you anymore.

**Forgiveness Is a Gift to Yourself**

Forgiveness frees up your emotional and mental energy for more productive pursuits.

Your identity is not defined by what someone did to you.

We've talked about what forgiveness is and what it isn't.

We're going to explore practical ways to manage emotions and find a way to forgive the person who offended or hurt you.

As impossible as it seems right now, through the forgiveness process, you're going to learn to release your anger toward that person.

You're going to learn to replace walls with boundaries.

You're going to reclaim your life.

**Moving Forward**

Remember, you're not trying to forgive all at once. You're just trying to break the anger cycle that's been keeping you stuck.

Each time you interrupt that cycle, you create space for healing to happen.

In the next part of this book, we'll go over specific tools to help you move through these steps... especially that second step where most people get stuck... anger.

You're not alone in this. And you're not going to stay stuck forever.

Let's keep moving forward together.

# 7

# WHERE YOU ARE RIGHT NOW

B y now you understand the four steps in the forgiveness process. You know what forgiveness means and what it doesn't mean. You know you can make the choice to move from walls to boundaries, from isolation to wisdom, and from fear to growth.

But understanding the forgiveness steps and actually walking through them are two completely different things. You likely need some help even thinking about how you can get past your anger.

This makes complete sense. Knowing these things and actually applying them in real life are separated by a gap that many people find difficult to cross. You can intellectually understand that forgiveness would benefit you while still feeling emotionally unable to forgive. That is very normal.

Let me describe where you probably are right now, because recognizing your current position is important before taking the next step.

## This Is Where Most People Are

At this point in their journey, most people find themselves thinking several things:

"I can see that I'm paying a high price for staying angry. The cost analysis opened my eyes to how much this is affecting my sleep, health, relationships, and peace of mind."

"I understand what forgiveness actually means now. It's not about excusing their behavior or becoming a doormat. It's about my own freedom."

"I know 'I can make the choice to tear down my walls and build boundaries instead. I understand that hiding behind walls isn't the same as having mature protection."

"I can identify where I am in the four steps of the forgiveness process. I'm clearly stuck in step two... I'm angry! I've been camping out there for a long time."

"But I still have absolutely no idea how to actually move through these steps. I have no idea how to stop being so angry. The idea of forgiveness in this situation still seems impossible. Understanding forgiveness and being able to forgive feel like two completely different things."

If that's where you are, you're in exactly the right place. This is where most people find themselves after learning about forgiveness.

## This Is Normal... And It Doesn't Mean You're Failing

You feel angry. You likely feel stuck, though you might just be realizing how stuck you actually are. You feel like forgiveness is impossible.

This is completely normal.

This is where everyone struggles. Absolutely everyone. This is the most common place for people to get stuck in the forgiveness process.

**Most people stay stuck in anger.** Maybe for months or years. Some people stay there for decades. Some people never move past it.

The fact that you feel angry doesn't mean you're doing something wrong. The fact that forgiveness feels impossible doesn't mean you're incapable of it. The fact that you can't imagine how to move forward doesn't mean there isn't a way forward.

It just means you're human, and you're dealing with a genuinely difficult situation in the most natural way possible.

Your anger makes sense. Your resistance makes sense. Your confusion makes sense.

What you're feeling is not only normal... it's evidence that what happened to you mattered. If you could just shrug it off and move on, it might mean either the offense wasn't that serious or you don't value yourself enough to be upset when you're mistreated.

Your anger is proof that you have standards. Your struggle with forgiveness is proof that you take relationships seriously.

Don't judge yourself for being where you are. You're exactly where most people would be if they had been through what you've been through.

### The Gap Between Knowing and Doing

You are beginning to understand that there are steps you can take that can bring you healing and freedom.

But here's the thing... understanding something intellectually doesn't automatically make it emotionally achievable.

You can know that exercise is good for you and still struggle to get to the gym. You can understand that a healthy diet will improve your life and still find yourself eating junk food. You can recognize that forgiveness would benefit you and still feel unable to forgive.

This gap between knowing and doing isn't a character flaw. It's part of being human.

The solution isn't to understand forgiveness better. You already understand it well enough. The solution is to develop practical skills that help you bridge the gap between what you know and what you can actually do.

You've made the choice to tear down walls and build boundaries. Now you need the tools to actually make that happen. You need specific techniques to help you move from anger toward healing.

That's what part two of this book is about... giving you specific, practical tools that work when understanding alone isn't enough.

### Where You Need to Go Next

You don't need more theory about forgiveness. You understand it well enough already.

You don't need more reasons why forgiveness would be good for you. You're already convinced it would benefit you.

You don't need more examples of other people who have forgiven in difficult circumstances. You believe it's possible.

What you need now are practical tools that help you move forward when you're feeling stuck.

You need healthy coping mechanisms that help you interrupt the anger cycle while you work through the forgiveness process.

You need strategies that actually work when your emotions are telling you that forgiveness is impossible.

You need skills that bridge the gap between understanding forgiveness and being able to practice it.

Part two of this book provides exactly that. We're going to start with healthy coping mechanisms... the specific healthy techniques you can use when anger threatens to overwhelm you. Then we'll move into the deeper work of actually processing and releasing the hurt.

## You Have More Control Than You May Realize

Here's something that might surprise you... you have more control over this situation than you think you do.

You can't control what was done to you. That already happened.

You can't control whether they apologize, change, or face consequences for their actions. Those things are up to them and the natural course of events.

But you can control how much longer what they did controls your daily experience.

You can control whether you continue to give them free rent in your head.

You can control whether you keep paying the high price of anger and resentment.

You can control whether you choose to work toward forgiveness or stay stuck where you are.

That control might not feel real to you right now because your emotions are so strong. But it's there. And part two of this book will show you how to exercise it.

## The Reality Check

Let's be honest about where you are right now, **you just can't forgive that.**

Not yet.

But "yet" is the key word in that sentence.

You just can't forgive that yet. But you can learn to forgive it. You can develop the skills necessary to work through the forgiveness process. You can find ways to manage your emotions while you do the work of healing.

The word "yet" implies that change is possible. It suggests that your current inability to forgive is temporary, not permanent.

"I just can't forgive that" feels hopeless and final.

"I just can't forgive that yet" acknowledges your current reality while leaving room for growth.

You're not stuck forever. You're stuck for now.

**The Promise**

You don't have to stay where you are.

You don't have to be controlled by what someone else did to you.

You don't have to carry this weight for the rest of your life.

You can learn to forgive, even when it feels impossible.

You can reclaim your peace, your joy, and your freedom.

You can get your life back.

The tools exist. The path is marked. Other people have walked it successfully.

Your healing is possible.

Your freedom is within reach.

You just need to know how to get there.

Let's figure that out together.

# PART II

---

# GETTING STARTED WITH FORGIVENESS

# 8

---

# TIME TO MOVE FORWARD

You now know there's a process for forgiveness... the four steps that people naturally move through. You've learned what forgiveness means and what it doesn't mean. You've been presented the choice to move from walls to boundaries, from hiding to wisdom, from isolation to self-protection.

If you're like most people, you're still stuck in Step Two... you're angry. You've probably been there for months. Maybe years. Maybe decades. It's possible that you're just coming to realize that at some point you built walls to protect yourself and you've never taken them down. You probably sense that anger is costing you more than it's benefiting you. You know you're not living as fully as you could be.

The fog may be clearing. You might be able to see there is a bridge from anger to freedom, but you don't know how to cross it. The gap between understanding forgiveness and actually forgiving feels enormous.

You're not alone in this struggle. Most people get stuck exactly where you are right now. Knowing what forgiveness is doesn't automatically give you the ability to forgive. You're human. You have feelings. You've been hurt. Understanding there is a forgiveness process doesn't make the process easy. You probably feel like you need a little help to get moving, to start crossing the bridge to forgiveness. For you. So you can live your life fully.

This part of the book provides the practical tools you need to move forward. We're going to help you learn what you need to learn from your anger, then move through it toward healing. We're not asking you to forgive everything at once. We're asking you to take the next step in your journey toward freedom.

Let's first take a few moments to understand why anger is useful in the short term and then look at why it is important to move beyond your anger.

# 9

# UNDERSTANDING YOUR ANGER

B efore we ask you to release your anger, let's first discuss what you're actually being asked to let go of.

This isn't about judging anger as bad or wrong. Anger serves important purposes, and your anger about what happened to you probably makes complete sense.

But anger can also become a trap. Understanding how anger works... both its benefits and its costs... will help you make informed decisions about when anger is serving you and when it's enslaving you.

Your anger feels justified because it probably is justified. Someone wronged you. They violated your trust, hurt you, or damaged something important to you. Your anger is evidence that you have standards, that you value yourself enough to be upset when you're mistreated.

But justified anger and helpful anger aren't always the same thing.

## Why Anger Feels Good and Righteous

Anger feels good for several important reasons:

**Anger validates that you matter.** When someone hurts you and you feel angry, that anger confirms that you're worth protecting. It says that you don't deserve to be treated poorly and that what happened to you was wrong. In a world where people sometimes minimize your pain or tell you to "get over it," anger validates that your feelings matter.

**Anger provides a sense of moral superiority.** When you're angry at someone who wronged you, you get to be the good guy in the story. You're the victim; they're the villain. You're righteous; they're wrong. This moral high ground feels powerful and important, especially when you've been made to feel powerless by what they did.

**Anger gives you energy when you might otherwise feel powerless.** Hurt can make you feel weak, vulnerable, and defeated. Anger transforms that powerless feeling into something that feels stronger. Instead of feeling like a victim, anger helps you feel like a fighter. Instead of collapsing under the weight of what happened, anger gives you the energy to keep going.

**Anger creates distance from vulnerability and pain.** It's easier to be angry than to feel the deeper emotions underneath... the hurt, the disappointment, the grief over what was lost. Anger feels more powerful than sadness. It feels more active than despair. It protects you from having to fully feel the depth of what was done to you.

**Anger feels like justice when there's no actual justice.** If the person who hurt you hasn't faced consequences, your anger feels like the only thing holding them accountable. Your anger feels like evidence that what they did was wrong. Without your anger, it might feel like they're getting away with it completely.

All of these functions of anger make complete sense. Anger isn't irrational or wrong. It's a natural, protective response to being hurt.

## The Biochemical Payoff of Anger

Anger doesn't just feel good emotionally... it creates actual chemical rewards in your brain and body.

When you get angry, your body releases stress hormones like adrenaline and cortisol. These chemicals trigger your fight-or-flight response, which can feel energizing and powerful. Your heart rate increases, your muscles tense, your focus sharpens. You feel ready for action.

This biochemical response can be temporarily rewarding. The adrenaline rush can feel good, especially if you've been feeling depressed, numb, or powerless. Some people become unconsciously addicted to this chemical high that anger provides.

The brain also releases other chemicals during anger that can create a sense of reward or satisfaction. When you rehearse how wrong the other person was, when you build your case against them, when you imagine confronting them, your brain can release small hits of satisfaction chemicals.

But like any chemical high, the anger rush eventually crashes. When the adrenaline and cortisol wear off, you're often left feeling depleted, exhausted, or empty. This crash can make you crave the anger high again, creating a cycle that's hard to break.

Over time, chronic anger and the stress hormones it produces can damage your physical health. Chronic anger is linked to heart disease, high blood pressure, weakened immune system, and other serious health problems.

## How Anger Becomes a Habit and Addiction

Your brain learns through repetition. Every time you think angry thoughts, you're strengthening the neural pathways that make angry thinking easier and more automatic.

Think of it like walking through a field. The first time you walk across the field, you have to push through tall grass and create a path. The second time, the path is a little clearer. The more times you walk the same path, the more established it becomes, until eventually you have a clear trail that's easy to follow.

The same thing happens with anger. The more you rehearse angry thoughts, the more automatic they become. The more you focus on what the other person did wrong, the easier it becomes to find new things to be angry about. The more you replay the offense in your mind, the more vivid and immediate it feels.

Eventually, anger can become your default emotional response to stress, disappointment, or conflict. Instead of feeling hurt, you feel angry. Instead of feeling sad, you feel angry. Instead of feeling scared, you feel angry. Anger becomes your go-to emotion because it's the path your brain has been trained to follow.

This is when anger crosses the line from being a natural response to being an addiction. You're not choosing anger anymore... anger is choosing you.

Some people become so accustomed to anger that peace feels uncomfortable or foreign. They don't know who they are without something to be angry about. They don't know how to process emotions without the energy that anger provides.

### Why We Get Stuck in the Anger Phase

Even when anger stops serving us, we often resist letting it go for several important reasons:

**Anger feels like the only thing honoring the offense.** You might worry that if you stop being angry, it means what happened to you didn't matter. Your anger feels like the only thing keeping the offense "alive" and acknowledging its significance.

**Anger feels like protection from future hurt.** If you stay angry, you stay alert to danger. If you let go of anger, you might let your guard down and get hurt again. Anger feels like armor that keeps you safe.

**Anger keeps the offender "accountable" in your mind.** Even if they never face real consequences, your anger feels like it's holding them responsible. Your anger feels like the only thing preventing them from completely getting away with what they did.

**Moving past anger feels like giving up your righteous position.** If you're no longer angry, you're no longer clearly the victim and they're no longer clearly the villain. The moral clarity that anger provides feels important to maintain.

**Anger feels more powerful than other emotions.** Hurt feels weak. Sadness feels vulnerable. Disappointment feels passive. Anger feels strong and active and in control.

**Letting go of anger feels like letting go of justice.** If you're not angry anymore, who's going to remember what they did? Who's going to care that you were wronged? Your anger feels like the only form of justice available.

## The Difference Between Justified Anger and Destructive Anger

Not all anger is created equal. There's an important difference between anger that serves you and anger that enslaves you.

### Justified, functional anger:

- Responds to a real wrong or injustice

- Motivates you to take protective action

- Helps you set boundaries and stand up for yourself

- Gives you energy to make necessary changes

- Fades naturally once the situation is addressed

• Doesn't consume your daily life or relationships

**Destructive, dysfunctional anger:**

• Becomes your primary identity or way of relating to the world

• Controls your daily emotional experience

• Doesn't lead to any productive action or positive change

• Affects your relationships with people who weren't involved in the offense

• Continues long after any protective function has been served

• Costs you more than it benefits you

Here's the key question... Is your anger still serving a protective function, or has it become a prison?

Justified anger has a purpose and a timeline. It motivates you to protect yourself, set boundaries, or address the situation. Once you've taken appropriate action, justified anger naturally begins to fade.

Destructive anger has no end point. It feeds on itself. It looks for new evidence to support itself. It becomes a way of life rather than a response to a specific situation.

You can have been completely justified in your initial anger while recognizing that your current anger has become destructive. The fact that they wronged you doesn't mean that staying angry forever serves your best interests.

### Recognizing When Anger Has Become Destructive

How do you know when your justified anger has crossed the line into destructive anger? Here are some warning signs:

**Your anger affects relationships with people who weren't involved.**

If you're taking out your anger about one person on everyone else in your life, your anger has become destructive.

**You spend more time thinking about the offense than you spend thinking about your current life.** If the offense occupies more mental space than your present relationships, goals, and activities, your anger has become destructive.

**Your anger hasn't motivated any positive changes.** If you've been angry for months or years without taking any protective action or making any beneficial changes, your anger isn't serving its protective function anymore.

**You feel worse, not better, after anger episodes.** If rehearsing your anger leaves you feeling depleted, bitter, or hopeless rather than energized and empowered, your anger has become destructive.

**You're angry about things that happened years ago as if they happened yesterday.** If old offenses feel as fresh and immediate as recent ones, you've gotten stuck in destructive anger patterns.

**You resist anything that might reduce your anger.** If the thought of letting go of your anger feels wrong or dangerous, your anger may have become an addiction rather than a tool.

### Breaking Free from Destructive Anger

Recognizing that your anger has become destructive doesn't mean you have to let go of it all at once. But it does mean you can start making different choices about how much power you give it over your life.

Remember the choice we talked about in Chapter 4... the choice to tear down walls and build boundaries. That's what we're talking about here. Moving from anger-as-armor (walls) to wisdom-based protection (boundaries).

You can acknowledge that you were wronged without rehearsing that wrong every day.

You can remember what happened without reliving it constantly.

You can protect yourself without staying in a constant state of anger.

You can honor the significance of what happened to you without letting it define your entire life.

The goal isn't to pretend you were never hurt or to minimize what happened to you. The goal is to prevent the hurt from continuing to hurt you every day.

Your anger served important purposes when it first showed up. It validated your worth, energized you to protect yourself, and acknowledged that what happened was wrong.

But anger that helped you survive the initial crisis can become a barrier to thriving in your ongoing life.

You have the power to thank your anger for how it protected you and then choose something different for your future.

You have the power to keep the lessons anger taught you while releasing the daily burden of carrying it.

You have the power to honor what happened to you by refusing to let it keep happening to you through your own thoughts and emotions.

Understanding your anger is the first step toward choosing what to do with it. You're not a victim of your anger... you're the one who gets to decide how much space it takes up in your life going forward.

Now, let's take a look at how we can begin to break the anger cycle and get back to living life fully.

# 10

# BREAKING THE ANGER CYCLE

D o you remember when we talked about Step Two in the forgiveness process... anger? We discussed how this is where most people get stuck for months or even years. We also talked about how anger serves important purposes initially, but becomes destructive when it becomes a permanent residence rather than a temporary shelter.

Well, now we're going to give you some practical ideas to help you move through that anger.

Forgiveness is for you. To get to forgiveness, you're going to have to find ways to move through your anger. That may seem impossible. It isn't. There are ways to break the anger cycle that's been keeping you trapped. This is where learning to use healthy coping mechanisms comes in. These help you to get started, to change direction, when you're learning to break free from destructive anger.

## What Is a Healthy Coping Mechanism?

A healthy coping mechanism is simply a strategy or technique that helps you manage difficult emotions or situations. When it comes to forgiveness, coping mechanisms are tools that help you interrupt the anger patterns that keep you stuck and create space for healing to happen.

Think of coping mechanisms like circuit breakers in your home's electrical system. Maybe you were running the microwave and toaster at the same time and the power went out. You had to go to the electrical panel and turn the switch back on. Once you reset the circuit breaker, you finish toasting your bread before you turn the microwave on again. When there's too much emotional current flowing through your system, these healthy coping mechanisms help prevent overload and give you a chance to reset.

The good news is that you probably already use healthy coping mechanisms without realizing it. Maybe you go for walks when you're stressed, or call a friend when you're upset, or organize your space when you feel out of control. We're going to build on that natural tendency by giving you specific tools designed to help with the anger cycle.

### Figure Out What Is Most Likely to Work For You

As you read through these coping mechanisms, remember that you don't have to use all of them. Some will resonate with you immediately, while others might feel wrong for your situation or your personality. Use what is helpful and leave what isn't for another time. You might even find that a mechanism you initially rejected becomes useful later as you grow and change through the forgiveness process.

Understanding how you naturally process difficult situations will help you choose the most effective tools for your journey toward forgiveness.

**Quick Assessment: How Do You Naturally Handle Problems?**

Before we dive into specific techniques, let's figure out your natural problem-solving style. This will help you know where to start.

Think about a recent challenge you faced (not related to forgiveness). How did you handle it?

Check the statements that sound most like you:

**Group A - The Thinker:**

☐ I thought through the problem step by step

☐ I researched solutions or asked for advice

☐ I made lists of pros and cons

☐ I needed to understand "why" this happened

**Group B - The Feeler:**

☐ I talked to friends about how I was feeling

☐ I needed time to process my emotions

☐ I trusted my gut feeling about what to do

☐ I felt better after expressing my feelings

**Group C - The Doer:**

☐ I jumped into action to fix the problem

☐ I changed my routine or environment immediately

☐ I focused on what I could control

☐ I felt better when I was doing something productive

**Group D - The Planner:**

☐ I created a plan with specific steps

☐ I scheduled time to deal with the problem

□ I felt better when I had a clear system to follow

□ I needed predictable ways to handle the situation

**What Your Results Mean**

If you checked mostly **Group A**, you're a cognitive processor who benefits from understanding and analyzing. You'll probably connect most with techniques that help you reframe thoughts and examine beliefs.

If you checked mostly **Group B**, you're an emotional processor who needs to feel and express. You'll likely respond well to techniques that help you release and process emotions.

If you checked mostly **Group C**, you're a physical processor who needs movement and action. You'll probably find the most relief in techniques that engage your body and create tangible change.

If you checked mostly **Group D**, you're a structured processor who thrives on systems and routines. You'll likely benefit most from techniques you can schedule and practice consistently.

**Finding Your Combination**

You might find that you use techniques from multiple categories, or that your needs change depending on the situation. Some days you might need the logical approach of cognitive processing, while other days you might need emotional release techniques. This is normal and healthy.

The goal isn't to eliminate anger completely... anger serves important purposes. The goal is to find coping mechanisms that help you stop and consider if your anger is serving you or if you are serving your anger. You will be amazed at how powerful it feels to be able to stop your anger and evaluate if it is still serving your best interests.

## Getting Started

Start with one or two techniques that feel most natural to you. Practice them consistently for a week before adding others. Building these skills takes time, but each time you successfully break an anger cycle, you're building your capacity for forgiveness.

Remember, you're not trying to forgive all at once. You're just trying to break the anger cycle that's been keeping you stuck. Each time you interrupt that cycle, you create space for healing to happen.

### *Start with What is Likely to Work Best for You*

Now that you've completed the Quick Assessment, let's see where it may be best for you to get started with when learning to use coping mechanisms to reduce your feelings of anger. Remember, the goal is to find what resonates with you and to get started.

**If you checked mostly Group A:** You may want to start with the section on Cognitive Processor techniques

**If you checked mostly Group B:** You may want to start with the section on Emotional Processor techniques

**If you checked mostly Group C:** You may want to start with the section on Action-Oriented techniques

**If you checked mostly Group D:** You may want to start with the section on Routine-Based techniques

**Not sure which fits?** You can always start with the Universal Cycle Breakers because they are likely to work for everyone.

Now, let's look at some coping mechanisms and work out which ones will likely work best for you.

### *For Cognitive Processors (For People who Think Their Way Out)*

You're someone who naturally analyzes situations and looks for logical solutions. When you're angry, you might replay conversations in your head, build cases against people, or get stuck in mental loops trying to "figure out" what happened. Your strength is your ability to reason through problems, but this can become a trap when you over-analyze emotional situations.

### "It Is What It Is"

This simple phrase helps you accept reality without fighting it. When you catch yourself trying to mentally change what happened or wishing things were different, remind yourself, "It is what it is." This doesn't mean you approve of what happened or that you're giving up. It means you're accepting that what's done is done, and your energy is better spent on what you can actually control.

### "Their Behavior Is Information About Them, Not Me"

When someone hurts you, it's natural to wonder what you did wrong or how you could have prevented it. This thinking trap keeps you focused on the offense and gives the other person continued power over your peace of mind. Instead, remind yourself that their choices reflect their character, values, and emotional state... not your worth or value.

### The "Information vs. Ammunition" Check

When you catch yourself thinking about what they did, ask yourself, "Am I gathering this information to protect myself, or am I stockpiling ammunition to use against them?" If you're building a case for future arguments or planning revenge, you're probably stuck in the anger cycle. If you're learning from the situation to make better decisions going forward, you're processing productively.

### The "Court Case" Technique

Write out your case against them as if you're presenting it to a judge. Include all the evidence of their wrongdoing. Then write their potential defense, what would their lawyer argue? This exercise often reveals that the situation is more complex than your anger makes it seem, helping you move from black-and-white thinking to a more nuanced understanding.

## Time-Boxing Anger Thoughts

Allow yourself 15 minutes per day to think about what happened. Set a timer. When angry thoughts come outside that designated time, remind yourself, "I'll think about this during my scheduled time." This prevents anger from taking over your entire day while still giving you space to process.

## "Let Them" Thinking

This technique from Mel Robbins involves accepting other people's choices instead of fighting them mentally. When you catch yourself upset about their behavior, practice saying, "They're choosing to be dishonest... let them." "They're refusing to apologize... let them." "They're spreading lies about me... let them." This redirects your energy from trying to control them to focusing on what you can control.

### *For Emotional Processors (For People Who Feel Their Way Through)*

You experience emotions deeply and need to feel your way through difficult situations rather than think your way out. When you're angry, you might feel overwhelmed by the intensity of your emotions or struggle to separate your feelings from reality. Your strength is your emotional intelligence and capacity for empathy.

## "Maybe They're Doing the Best They Can Right Now"

This doesn't excuse their behavior or minimize your hurt. It simply acknowledges that people often act badly when they're struggling, scared, or emotionally immature. You can think of times when your "best" wasn't very good because you were overwhelmed, stressed, or hurt. This perspective can soften your anger without requiring you to approve of what they did.

### Gratitude Bridging

When you feel anger rising, immediately name three things you're grateful for. This isn't about minimizing your hurt, but about reminding your brain that good things still exist alongside the pain. It breaks the cycle of negative thinking and helps regulate your emotional state.

### "I've Been the Villain in Someone Else's Story"

Remember times when you hurt someone, either intentionally or accidentally. How did you want to be treated afterward? What grace did you need? This doesn't mean their actions were acceptable, but it can help you remember that all of us are capable of causing pain and all of us need forgiveness sometimes.

### Emotion Labeling

Instead of saying "I'm angry," get specific... "I'm feeling betrayed and powerless." Or "I'm hurt and disappointed." This helps you process what's actually happening emotionally rather than getting stuck in general anger. When you can name the specific emotions, they often lose some of their power over you.

### Physical Release Rituals

Go for a walk while mentally "dropping off" your anger at specific locations along your route. Write angry letters you'll never send and then burn them safely. Do intense exercise while imagining you're releasing the negative energy. Your body holds anger physically, so physical release can be particularly effective for emotional processors.

### The "Both/And" Practice

Instead of either/or thinking, practice "both/and"... "I can both be hurt by what they did AND recognize they might have been struggling too." "I can both need time to heal AND choose to work toward forgiveness." This allows for complex feelings instead of black-and-white thinking.

### For Action-Oriented People (For People Who Do Something Different)

You prefer to solve problems through action rather than analysis or emotional processing. When you're angry, you might want to confront the person immediately or take some kind of action to "fix" the situation. Your strength is your ability to make changes and move forward, but you might struggle with situations where direct action isn't possible or helpful.

### Channel Redirection

When anger energy builds up, immediately redirect it into something productive. Go for a run, organize a closet, help someone else with their problems, or work on a project. The key is to use that angry energy for something constructive rather than letting it simmer or turn into destructive action.

### The "Stop Sign" Method

Choose a physical cue (like putting your hand up like a stop sign) to interrupt anger thoughts, then immediately do a different activity for 10 minutes. This could be calling a friend, doing jumping jacks, or working on a puzzle. The goal is to break the anger cycle before it gains momentum.

### Boundary Actions

Instead of trying to change them or get them to apologize, take concrete steps to protect yourself. Block their phone number, unfollow them on social media, change your routines to avoid them, or create physical distance. Focus on what you can control rather than what you can't.

### Help Someone Else

When you're stuck in anger about your situation, find someone else who needs help. Volunteer, help a neighbor, or support a friend going through difficulties. This shifts your focus from what was done to you to what you can do for others, breaking the cycle of self-focused anger.

### "Let Them" Actions

Practice stepping back from their drama. "They want to argue... let them argue with someone else." "They're trying to make me look bad... let them, while I focus on being the person I want to be." This preserves your energy for productive action rather than reactive behavior.

### *For Routine-Based People (For People Who Need Structure)*

You function best with clear systems and predictable patterns. When someone disrupts your sense of order through their actions, you might feel particularly unsettled. Your strength is your consistency and ability to build sustainable habits, but you might struggle with the unpredictable nature of forgiveness work.

### Daily Forgiveness Check-ins

At the same time each day, rate your anger level (1-10) and your willingness to forgive (1-10). Keep a simple log. Track patterns over time to see progress you might not otherwise notice. This gives you concrete data about your emotional journey.

### Scheduled Worry Time

Set aside 20 minutes daily to think about what happened. Use a timer. Outside that time, remind yourself, "I'll deal with this during my scheduled time." This contains the emotional processing to a specific time slot rather than letting it take over your entire day.

### Replacement Routines

If certain activities trigger memories of the offense, create new routines to replace them. If you used to call that person every Sunday, establish a new Sunday routine. If certain places remind you of what happened, find new places to go. This gives you control over your environment and associations.

**Progressive Exposure Practice**

Gradually reduce the amount of time you spend thinking about the offense each week. If you currently spend two hours daily thinking about it, reduce to 1 hour and 50 minutes this week, then 1 hour and 40 minutes next week. This systematic approach makes the process feel manageable.

**Structured "Let Them" Practice**

Create a daily list of things that are bothering you about this person or situation. Practice saying "let them" about each item. "They're posting happy pictures on social media after what they did... let them." "They're acting like nothing happened... let them." This systematic approach helps you practice releasing control.

*Universal Cycle Breakers (These Work for Everyone)*

These techniques can help anyone break the anger cycle, regardless of personality type:

**The 24-Hour Rule**

When you feel angry and want to take action (send a text, make a call, post on social media), commit to waiting 24 hours. Often the urgency fades, and you can respond more thoughtfully if you still choose to respond at all.

**Pattern Interrupts**

Develop a specific response for when you notice anger building. Count backward from 100, name five things you can see, do ten jumping jacks, or call a trusted friend. The key is to interrupt the anger pattern before it takes over.

### The "How Is This Serving Me?" Question

When you catch yourself in anger, ask honestly, "What benefit am I getting from staying angry, and is that benefit worth the cost?" Sometimes anger feels powerful or helps you avoid other painful emotions. Recognizing what anger is doing for you helps you find healthier ways to meet those needs.

### The "What Would Love Do?" Question

When you're stuck in anger, ask, "What would love do in this situation?" This doesn't mean being a doormat or accepting mistreatment. It means choosing the response that serves your highest good and reflects the person you want to be.

### Prayer

If prayer is part of your life, use it when you're stuck in anger.

This might seem obvious, but many people forget to pray about their anger. They pray about their hurt, their confusion, their need for healing... but they don't specifically ask for help with the anger itself.

When anger overwhelms you, pray for:

• Wisdom to see the situation clearly

• Strength to choose healing over bitterness

• The ability to set healthy boundaries

• Freedom from the thoughts that keep you trapped

If prayer isn't part of your life, that's okay. The other techniques in this chapter will serve you well. There's a chapter at the end of this book that explores the spiritual dimension of forgiveness, if you're curious about that perspective.

## Moving Forward

Now that you've found healthy coping mechanisms to interrupt the anger cycle, you're ready for the next step.

Using healthy coping mechanisms to break the anger pattern creates space. Space to think more clearly. Space to feel something other than rage. Space to consider what comes next.

But here's what often happens in that space... you realize you've been holding onto more than just anger. You've been holding onto contempt. You've hardened your heart not just against what they did, but against who they are as a person.

This hardening served a purpose, it protected you. But like the walls we talked about earlier, this protection can become a prison. There comes a time when this is no longer serving you.

The next step isn't about trusting them again or letting them back into your life. Remember, forgiveness can leave space for reconciliation. But, you don't have to move on to reconciliation.

The key is to focus on opening your heart safely... with boundaries intact... so you can live fully again.

Let's talk about how to do that.

## 11

# OPENING YOUR HEART SAFELY

When someone hurts you deeply, something happens beyond just anger. Your heart hardens. You shut down emotionally. You build walls. You decide that this person... and maybe people in general.. can't be trusted.

This emotional shutdown serves a purpose. It protects you from immediate further harm. It gives you distance from the pain. It keeps you safe while you're most vulnerable.

But there comes a time when you need to make a choice... Will you let your heart open again?

Opening your heart doesn't mean going back to being naive. It doesn't mean dropping your guard or trusting people who've proven untrustworthy. It doesn't mean pretending the hurt didn't happen. It doesn't mean reconciling with or even spending time around the person who hurt you.

It means choosing to live fully again, with wisdom and boundaries intact.

This chapter will help you learn to protect yourself in a way that allows you to live your life fully. You're not opening your heart completely... you're opening it safely, wisely, with protective boundaries in place.

## Understanding Contempt: When Your Heart Hardens

Before we talk about opening your heart, let's understand what happens when it closes completely. When someone hurts you, it's natural to feel angry. But sometimes anger hardens into something more destructive... contempt.

Contempt is different from anger. Anger is a response to what someone did. Contempt is a judgment about who someone is.

With anger, you're upset about their behavior. With contempt, you've decided they're worthless as a person.

With anger, you might change your mind if they change their behavior. With contempt, no matter what they do, you're not willing to reconsider your opinion of them.

Contempt feels powerful because it puts you in a position of superiority. You're good; they're bad. You're the victim; they're the villain. You're righteous; they're worthless.

But contempt is actually a trap. It keeps you emotionally tied to the person through your disdain for them. It also closes off any possibility of understanding, healing, or moving forward.

When you hold someone in contempt, you've essentially frozen them in time at their worst moment. You refuse to see them as anything other than the person who hurt you. This means they continue to have power over your emotional state, even when they're not in your life anymore.

Contempt also affects how you see the world. When you decide someone is completely bad, you start looking for evidence to support that belief. Every story you hear about them reinforces your contempt. Every memory you have gets filtered through your negative judgment.

Moving from contempt to curiosity is essential for your own freedom. You don't have to like them or trust them or have them in your life. But you do need to stop letting contempt control your emotional state.

## What Boundaries Actually Are

Before we talk about opening your heart safely, we need to understand what safety looks like. This is where boundaries come in... the same boundaries we discussed in Chapter 4.

Many people don't understand what boundaries actually are. They think boundaries are rules they set for other people. They're not.

Boundaries are limits you set on your own behavior to protect your physical, emotional, and mental well-being.

A boundary isn't... "You can't call me after 9 PM." A boundary is... "I won't answer my phone after 9 PM."

A boundary isn't... "You have to apologize before I'll talk to you." A boundary is... "I won't engage in conversation until you acknowledge what happened."

A boundary isn't... "You can't treat me that way." A boundary is... "I'll leave the room if you speak to me disrespectfully."

See the difference? Boundaries are about what you will or won't do, not about controlling what other people do.

This is actually liberating because it means you don't need anyone's permission to set boundaries. You don't need them to agree with your boundaries or understand them. You just need to decide what you will and won't accept, and then act accordingly.

**Permission to Protect Yourself**

If you need permission to set boundaries, you have it.

You have permission to protect your peace of mind.

You have permission to limit contact with people who consistently hurt you.

You have permission to end conversations that become abusive.

You have permission to say no to requests that violate your values or well-being.

You have permission to choose who gets access to your time, energy, and emotional space.

You don't have to justify these boundaries to anyone. You don't have to explain why you need them. You don't have to prove that you deserve to be treated well.

Setting boundaries isn't mean or selfish. It's responsible. It's taking care of yourself so you can be healthy enough to love others well.


**"Maybe They're Doing the Very Best They Can Right Now"**

This phrase might make you want to throw this book across the room. "The best they can? They can do better than that! They destroyed my life! They betrayed my trust! They hurt me on purpose!"

I understand that reaction. But stay with me for a moment.

Think about a time in your life when your "best" wasn't very good. Maybe you were overwhelmed, exhausted, or dealing with your own pain. Maybe you made choices you normally wouldn't make because you were scared, angry, or desperate.

Maybe you said things you didn't mean because you were hurt. Maybe you failed to show up for someone because you were barely keeping your own life together. Maybe you made a decision that seemed right at the time but caused damage you didn't intend.

In those moments, you were doing the best you could with the emotional, mental, and spiritual resources you had available. That doesn't excuse the harm you caused, but it explains it.

The same might be true for the person who hurt you.

Maybe they were raised in a home where betrayal was normal. Maybe they were dealing with their own trauma or mental health struggles. Maybe they were so afraid of being hurt that they hurt you first. Maybe they were so emotionally immature that they couldn't handle the responsibility of the relationship.

This doesn't make what they did okay. It doesn't minimize the damage they caused. It doesn't mean you should trust them again or let them back into your life.

But it might help you understand that their actions were more about their limitations than about your worth.

When you can see their behavior as evidence of their brokenness rather than evidence of your inadequacy, it becomes easier to release the personal sting of what they did.

### The 80/20 Rule

This concept comes from recognizing that most people aren't entirely good or entirely bad, they're a mixture of both.

If someone in your life is doing 80% of things right and 20% of things wrong, you have a choice about where to focus your attention. You can spend all your emotional energy on the 20% they're doing wrong, building a case against them and collecting evidence of their failures. Or you can acknowledge the 80% they're doing right while addressing the 20% that needs to change.

This rule can be applied to the person who hurt you, even in retrospect. Yes, they caused significant damage. But were there also times when they showed kindness, helped you, or treated you well?

This doesn't excuse the harm they caused. The 20% that was wrong might have been seriously wrong... betrayal, abuse, or abandonment. But remembering the 80% that wasn't actively harmful can help you see them as a complete person rather than just as the source of your pain.

Important caveat... this rule doesn't apply in situations involving abuse, ongoing harm, or safety concerns. If someone is actively dangerous, focus on protection, not on finding their positive qualities.

But for many situations, the 80/20 perspective can help you move from seeing them as entirely evil to seeing them as flawed.

## "Let Them" - Boundary Setting in Action

Remember the "Let Them" technique? This is actually boundary setting, even though it might not feel like it.

When you say, "They're choosing to be dishonest... let them," you're setting a boundary. You're deciding that you won't waste your energy trying to make them honest.

When you say, "They're refusing to apologize... let them," you're setting a boundary. You're deciding that your healing doesn't depend on their apology.

When you say, "They're spreading lies about me... let them," you're setting a boundary. You're deciding that you won't exhaust yourself trying to control their narrative.

Each "let them" statement is you taking back power over your own emotional state and your life. You're deciding what you will and won't engage with. You're choosing where to put your energy.

This is boundary setting without confrontation. You're not demanding that they change. You're just deciding that you won't let their choices control your choices.

## Moving from Contempt to Curiosity

Curiosity is the antidote to contempt.

Instead of deciding you know everything about why they did what they did, what if you got curious about their story?

"I wonder what was happening in their life when they made that choice?"

"I wonder what they were afraid of?"

"I wonder what pain they were carrying that made them act that way?"

"I wonder if they even realize how much damage they caused?"

Curiosity doesn't require you to excuse their behavior or reconcile with them. It just opens a door in your understanding that contempt had slammed shut.

Sometimes curiosity leads to understanding. Sometimes it just leads to sadness about how broken they must be to act the way they did. Either way, it's healthier for you than contempt.

Maintain your boundaries while being curious. You can wonder about their story without giving them access to yours. You can try to understand them without trusting them. You can be curious about their humanity without becoming vulnerable to their dysfunction.

## Building Bridges Without Excusing Behavior

Here's a crucial distinction... understanding someone's behavior is not the same as excusing it.

An explanation is not an excuse.

You can understand that someone betrayed you because they were insecure and afraid of abandonment without excusing the betrayal.

You can understand that someone lied to you because they were trying to protect themselves without excusing the lie.

You can understand that someone hurt you because they themselves were hurt without excusing the damage they caused.

Understanding creates a bridge between your anger and your healing. It allows you to start living your life fully.

It allows you to see them as human without trusting them again. It permits compassion without demanding reconciliation.

The goal isn't to justify what they did. The goal is to understand enough to let go of contempt while maintaining the boundaries necessary to protect yourself.


## When Opening Your Heart Becomes Dangerous

There's a difference between opening your heart safely and opening it naively.

Opening your heart safely means choosing to understand while maintaining appropriate boundaries.

Opening your heart naively means making excuses for genuinely harmful behavior and putting yourself at risk for more harm.

Warning signs that you're moving toward dangerous territory:

• You find yourself minimizing serious harm they caused

• You're making excuses for ongoing bad behavior

• You're considering trusting them again before they've shown genuine change

• You're taking responsibility for their choices

• You're ignoring red flags because you want to believe they've changed

• You're dropping boundaries because you feel guilty for having them

If you notice these patterns, step back and focus on protection rather than understanding.

Remember: you can forgive someone while still recognizing that they're not safe for you to be around. You can have compassion for their brokenness while refusing to let their brokenness break you.

### Practical Exercises for Opening Your Heart Safely

### The Humanizing Exercise

Write about the person who hurt you as if you were describing them to someone who had never met them. Include both positive and negative qualities. What would a balanced, honest description look like?

This exercise helps you see them as a complete person rather than just as the source of your pain.

### Boundary Clarity Exercise

Write down three boundaries you need to maintain with this person, even if you forgive them. For each boundary, write:

• What the boundary is (what you will or won't do)

• Why this boundary is necessary for your well-being

• How you will maintain this boundary

This exercise helps you understand that forgiveness and boundaries can coexist.

### The "What If" Questions

Ask yourself these questions without requiring yourself to find answers:

• What if they were doing the best they could with the emotional resources they had?

• What if they were acting out of fear rather than malice?

• What if they didn't realize how much damage they were causing?

• What if they're struggling with their own pain and brokenness?

The goal isn't to excuse their behavior but to create space for a more nuanced understanding.

**The Daily Curiosity Practice**

Once a day, instead of rehearsing what they did wrong, spend five minutes wondering about their story. What might have shaped them into someone who would act that way? What pain might they carry? What fears might drive their behavior?

This practice gradually shifts your heart from contempt toward curiosity while maintaining your boundaries.

**The Heart That Opens Safely**

Opening your heart safely is risky. It means choosing to feel when it would be safer to stay numb. It means choosing to understand when it would be easier to demonize. It means choosing hope when despair feels more justified.

But here's what happens when your heart opens safely... you become free.

Free from the exhausting work of maintaining contempt.

Free from the prison of seeing the world in black and white.

Free from being controlled by what someone else did to you.

Free to choose forgiveness not because they deserve it, but because you deserve freedom.

The person who hurt you may never change. They may never acknowledge what they did wrong. They may never ask for your forgiveness.

But your heart can open anyway.

Your heart can open safely, with wisdom and boundaries intact.

Your heart can choose understanding without approving of their actions.

Your heart can choose freedom, regardless of what they choose.

This is your choice. This is your power. This is your path to freedom.

It's time to start living your life fully again.

# 12

## THE FOUNDATION OF FORGIVENESS

**Y**our Work Is Complete

Before we go any further, I want to be absolutely clear about something.

The forgiveness work you've done is complete and valuable on its own.

You've learned to break free from anger. You've learned to protect yourself with boundaries instead of walls. You've learned practical tools to interrupt the cycles that kept you stuck. You've learned that forgiveness is FOR YOU, not for the person who hurt you.

That's real. That's powerful. That's yours.

For some of you, this is exactly what you needed, and your journey ends here. You have the tools. You have the freedom. You're ready to live your life fully.

I celebrate what you've accomplished. You've taken an amazing journey. You've done hard work. You've grown. You've chosen freedom over bondage. That is amazing. Well done!

## An Invitation to Explore

For some of you, there's something else stirring.

Maybe you've sensed there's something bigger at work in forgiveness. Maybe you're wondering why this process feels so profound, so transformative. Maybe you sense there's a spiritual piece to your own healing that you haven't fully explored yet.

If that's you, keep reading.

What follows is an invitation, not a requirement. It's a doorway for those who want to walk through it, not a wall blocking those who don't.

The forgiveness you've learned stands on its own. What I'm about to share is for those who want to understand the spiritual foundation of why forgiveness is so powerful.


## The Pattern You've Discovered

Throughout this book, you've learned that forgiveness is about canceling a debt.

When someone hurts you, they owe you something. An apology. An explanation. Restitution. Justice. Some form of payment for the damage they caused.

When you forgive them, you cancel that debt. You say, "You don't owe me anymore. I'm not going to keep trying to collect what you owe me. I'm releasing you from that obligation."

This doesn't mean what they did was free. It cost you something... your trust, your security, your peace of mind. But you chose to absorb that cost rather than continuing to try to collect payment from them.

Here's what I've discovered over 15 years of walking with people through forgiveness.

This isn't just a helpful psychological technique.

It's actually a reflection of something fundamental about how the universe works. About how God relates to us.


## Your Need for Forgiveness Too

You've learned to forgive others because you know you need forgiveness too.

You've hurt people. Sometimes intentionally. Sometimes accidentally. Sometimes because you were overwhelmed, scared, or dealing with your own pain.

You've said things you didn't mean. You've made choices that caused damage you didn't intend. You've failed to show up for people who needed you. You've let your own brokenness spill over onto others.

You've needed grace from them. And hopefully, they've given it to you.

The same is true in your relationship with God.

We've all done things we're not proud of. We've all hurt people. We've all fallen short of the person we want to be, the person God created us to be. We've all chosen to rebel against God.

We've all been selfish when we should have been generous. Harsh when we should have been kind. Closed when we should have been open. We've chosen our own comfort over others' needs. We've known the right thing to do and done the opposite anyway.

If God kept a record of all those wrongs... if He demanded full payment for every mistake, every selfish choice, every time we've hurt someone or rejected love... we'd be in debt we could never repay.

But that's not how God works.

Instead, He offers the same thing you've learned to offer others.

Forgiveness. Grace. A canceled debt.

## The Ultimate Example

Let me tell you about someone who demonstrated forgiveness at the deepest level.

His name was Jesus, and He lived a perfect life.

He never lied. Never cheated. Never betrayed anyone's trust. He spent His time helping people... healing the sick, feeding the hungry, comforting those who were grieving. He stood up for the marginalized. He challenged the powerful who were abusing their authority. He taught people how to live with love and integrity.

But the people He came to help turned on Him.

His friends abandoned Him when He needed them most. The religious leaders falsely accused Him because they thought He threatened their power. The government officials condemned Him to death even though they knew He was innocent. The crowd that had praised Him days earlier demanded His execution.

He was beaten. Mocked. Tortured. Nailed to a cross to die a slow, agonizing death.

As He hung there, suffering for crimes He didn't commit, betrayed by friends, abandoned by those He loved, He said something remarkable.

"Father, forgive them, for they don't know what they're doing."

He chose forgiveness when He had done absolutely nothing to deserve the treatment He received. He forgave the very people who were killing Him.

Think about that for a moment.

You've been working through forgiveness for someone who hurt you. Maybe they betrayed your trust. Maybe they lied to you. Maybe they damaged something important in your life.

Jesus was being executed for crimes He didn't commit... and He chose forgiveness.

But here's what makes this even more profound.

Jesus didn't just forgive those who hurt Him in that moment.

He willingly took the punishment for every wrong thing every person has ever done. Including you. Including me.

He absorbed the cost of all our betrayals, all our selfishness, all our cruelty, all our failures, all our rebellion.

He died so that we could be forgiven. He suffered so that we could be free. He was rejected so that we could be accepted.

Three days later, He rose from the dead.

That resurrection proved something crucial. It proved that love is more powerful than hatred. That forgiveness is more powerful than revenge. That life is more powerful than death. That grace is more powerful than guilt.

## How This Connects to Your Journey

God isn't holding your mistakes over your head, waiting for you to pay Him back.

He's not keeping a record of your wrongs and demanding an impossible payment.

He's not making you earn forgiveness through being good enough or trying hard enough.

Instead, He's offering you the same thing you've learned to offer others.

Forgiveness.

He's saying, "I love you despite what you've done. I want to forgive you and give you a fresh start. I want to have a relationship with you based on grace, not on your performance. I want to cancel the debt you could never pay."

This is the spiritual foundation underneath everything you've learned in this book.

You've been learning to forgive others the way God forgives you.

You've been learning to cancel debts the way your debt has been canceled.

You've been learning to offer grace the way grace has been offered to you.

## How to Receive God's Forgiveness

Receiving God's forgiveness requires the same humility you've had to develop in forgiving others.

You have to acknowledge that you've done things wrong and that you need forgiveness. Not because you're a terrible person, but because you're human, and humans hurt each other and fall short of who God meant us to be.

You have to believe that Jesus really did die to pay for your wrongdoing. That His sacrifice is sufficient to cover everything you've ever done wrong. That you don't have to earn forgiveness because it's already been offered.

You have to accept His gift of forgiveness instead of trying to pay Him back through being good enough.

You can do this right now, wherever you are, by simply talking to God.

There's nothing magical in these words, they are here to help you express what you may be thinking.

*"God, I know I've made mistakes and hurt both You and other people. I know I need forgiveness that I can't earn on my own. I believe that Jesus died to pay for my wrongdoing and rose again to give me new life. I accept Your gift of forgiveness. I want to live my life in relationship with You. Thank You for loving me enough to make a way for me to be forgiven."*

Do you feel it?

Your debt was canceled. Your relationship with God was restored. You became part of something bigger than yourself... a family of people who have been forgiven and are learning to live in that grace.

## An Additional Layer of Freedom

For those who choose to explore this spiritual dimension, something beautiful can happen.

When you're secure in God's forgiveness, it becomes even easier to forgive others.

When you know you're loved unconditionally by your Creator, other people's opinions and actions lose their power to control your peace.

When you know that you've been forgiven for every wrong thing you've ever done or ever will do, you can extend that same grace to others without feeling like you're letting them off the hook unfairly.

When you understand that God didn't wait for you to deserve forgiveness before offering it, you can forgive others without waiting for them to deserve it either.

This spiritual foundation doesn't replace the work you've done. It enhances it. It deepens it. It gives you an unshakeable source of peace that doesn't depend on your circumstances or other people's choices.

But I want to be clear about this.

This isn't required for the forgiveness work to be effective. The spiritual principle of forgiveness works no matter your relationship with God. Your freedom from anger and resentment is real whether you explore this spiritual dimension or not.

The tools you've learned work because they're based on truth about how humans process hurt and healing.

For those who want it, though, this spiritual foundation can add another layer of strength to your forgiveness practice. It can give you a source of grace that never runs dry, even when your own capacity for forgiveness feels exhausted.

### Your Journey Continues

Whether you choose to explore the spiritual dimension or not, your forgiveness journey is complete.

You don't have to carry the weight of anger and resentment anymore.

You don't have to pay the price of bitterness for the rest of your life.

You don't have to let what others have done to you determine how you live your life.

You can choose forgiveness... for others and for yourself.

You can choose freedom.

You can choose to live your life fully.

The choice is yours. It's always been yours.

Your heart can open safely again. Your life can be full again. Your future can be bright again.

Because forgiveness... both giving it and receiving it... really is the key to living fully.

## The Foundation of Freedom

The enemy's favorite strategy isn't to make you deny God. It's to keep you so busy with anger that you never focus on God. The enemy doesn't need you to stop believing. The enemy just needs you to stay distracted.

When you're consumed by what someone did to you, you're not focused on what God is doing in you. When your energy goes to resentment, it doesn't go to your calling.

Forgiveness isn't just emotional health. It's spiritual warfare. Every time you choose to forgive, you're refusing to let the enemy use your pain as a weapon against your purpose. You're breaking his strategy. You're taking back your focus.

This is why God commands forgiveness. Not because He's mean. Because He knows the enemy's playbook. And He's giving you the counter-strategy.

Forgive. Focus on God. Live free.

# ACKNOWLEDGMENTS

This book represents fifteen years of studying forgiveness and walking alongside people through their forgiveness process, combined with insights from thinkers, teachers, and recovery traditions whose work has shaped my understanding.

The four-step forgiveness process presented in Chapter 6 was inspired by Craig E. Johnson's work in Meeting the Ethical Challenges of Leadership: Casting Light or Shadow (SAGE Publications, 2012). While Johnson explored these steps in the context of organizational leadership, I've adapted and expanded them through years of practical application in pastoral counseling.

The concept of memory as a tool for reconciling our internal map with external reality comes from Dr. Jordan Peterson's lectures on psychology and meaning. His insights into how the brain processes unexpected events and updates our understanding of the world have been invaluable in helping people understand why offenses replay in their minds and when it's time to let them go.

Several foundational principles woven throughout this book... including "it is what it is," the acceptance of things beyond our control, and the recognition that people are simply doing the best they can with what they have... come from recovery wisdom I encountered during my own journey through a difficult season. These principles have proven themselves true in countless lives, including my own.

The "Let Them" and "80/20" techniques referenced in Chapters 10 and 11 comes from Mel Robbins, whose work on releasing control over others' choices has helped countless people find freedom from the exhausting work of trying to manage other people's behavior.

The discussion of anger's biochemical effects in Chapter 9 draws on established research in neuroscience and psychology about how stress hormones, neural pathways, and habit formation work. While I haven't cited specific studies, these concepts reflect current scientific understanding of how anger functions in the brain and body.

The emphasis on boundaries over walls, comparing anger and contempt, not being able to forgive yet, anger serves a purpose for a time but may not be serving you well now, the distinction between forgiveness and reconciliation, and that forgiveness opens the door to reconciliation but it doesn't require you to walk through it have emerged organically from thousands of hours of me sitting with real people working through real pain. Any wisdom in these pages has been tested in the crucible of human suffering and refined through watching people choose freedom over bondage.

I'm deeply grateful to everyone whose thinking has shaped mine, and especially to the hundreds of brave souls who trusted me to walk with them through forgiveness. Your courage made this book possible.

# ABOUT THE AUTHOR

 Keith West knows what it's like to be stuck in anger—not just from observing and helping others, but from his own difficult journey through hurt and forgiveness. After walking through his own process of healing, he's spent fifteen years studying forgiveness and sitting with hundreds of people who said, "I just can't forgive that"—and then watched them discover they could.

Keith doesn't offer Christian clichés or easy answers. He offers honest, practical tools that work whether you're deeply religious or not religious at all. His approach to forgiveness is simple. It's about getting your own life back.

After serving as a pastor at Reality Church in Papillion, Nebraska, Keith felt called to focus his efforts on building a ministry dedicated to forgiveness and healing. *I Just Can't Forgive That* is his first book, written for anyone exhausted by anger and ready for freedom... and for the pastors, counselors, and friends walking alongside them.

Keith lives in Bellevue, Nebraska, with his wife, Andrea, their six children, and grandchildren.

www.ingramcontent.com/pod-product-compliance
Lightning Source LLC
Chambersburg PA
CBHW060630130626
46555CB00002B/732